ALMOST PERSUADED

The Henry E. Sigerist Supplements to the
Bulletin of the History of Medicine
New Series, no. 1
Editor: Lloyd G. Stevenson

Henry E. Sigerist, recruited by William H. Welch to be director of the Johns Hopkins Institute of the History of Medicine, was the founder of the *Bulletin of the History of Medicine* and also of the first series of supplements, which extended from 1943 to 1951, when rising costs necessitated a pause in this important supplementary venture. That it can now be resumed, and a new series instituted, is due to the subsidy generously supplied by the American Association for the History of Medicine. It was Sigerist's resolve that the *Bulletin* should provide the organ not only of the Johns Hopkins Institute but also of the American Association, and to this day it subserves both functions. It is therefore eminently suitable that the new series should bear the founder's name and perpetuate his scholarly interests. These interests were so broad and so varied that the supplements will recognize no narrow limits in range of theme and will publish historical essays of greater scope than the *Bulletin* itself can accommodate. It is not too much to hope that in time the Sigerist supplements will help to extend the purview of medical history.

Protected!

From the *American Labor Legislation Review,* 1919, *9.*

ALMOST PERSUADED
AMERICAN PHYSICIANS AND COMPULSORY HEALTH INSURANCE, 1912-1920

Ronald L. Numbers

The Johns Hopkins University Press • Baltimore and London

Manufactured in the United States of America

The Johns Hopkins University Press, Baltimore, Maryland 21218
The Johns Hopkins Press Ltd., London

Library of Congress Catalog Card Number 77-17254
ISBN 0-8018-2052-9

Library of Congress Cataloging in Publication data will be found on the last printed page of this book.

To
Professor Maurice M. Vance
who first encouraged me to be a historian

CONTENTS

PREFACE

In 1911 the British parliament passed a National Insurance Act making health insurance mandatory for most employees between the ages of sixteen and seventy. The following year the American Association for Labor Legislation created a Committee on Social Insurance to prepare a model health-insurance bill for the United States, and by 1916 several state legislatures were actively considering bills that would have covered virtually all manual laborers earning $100 or less a month. No such law ever passed, but between 1916 and 1920 compulsory health insurance was a real possibility in a number of industrial states.

In this study of America's first debate over compulsory health insurance I focus primarily on the changing attitudes of the medical profession, leaving detailed analyses of labor, business, and political opinion to others. The initial response of physicians to compulsory health insurance was surprisingly positive. From the American Medical Association to various state and sectarian medical societies the feeling prevailed that this method of paying medical bills was both inevitable and desirable. By 1917, however, medical opinion was beginning to shift, and before long scarcely a physician could be found willing to endorse such a "socialistic" proposal.

In the absence of opinion polls it is impossible to determine precisely what American physicians were thinking at any given time. Nevertheless, a considerable body of opinion can be found in medical-society minutes, unpublished correspondence, and the numerous national, state, and local publications. When this literary evidence is combined with the votes of representative medical bodies, I think we can obtain a reasonably accurate reading of the prevailing views of the medical profession.

*   *   *

Much of the research for this study was done in 1973-74, while I was a Josiah Macy, Jr. Foundation Fellow in the History of Medicine and the Biological Sciences at the Institute of the History of Medicine, The Johns Hopkins University. Thus I owe an immense debt of gratitude to the Macy Foundation and to Lloyd G. Stevenson, the hospitable director of the Hopkins Institute, for making this volume possible. I am also grateful to Guenter B. Risse, former chairman of the Department of the History of Medicine, University of Wisconsin, for arranging a reduced teaching load in the fall of 1975 so that I could devote a substantial portion of my time to writing this monograph.

Among the many individuals who assisted me in locating and using various manuscript collections were: Richard Strassberg and Mary Arluck, of the Labor-Management Documentation Center, Cornell University; Marguerite Fallucco and Warren Albert, of the AMA's Archive-Library Department; Wesley Draper, of the Academy of Medicine of Brooklyn; Kathleen Jacklin, of the Cornell University Libraries; Dr. Adrian Lambert, of New York City; and Jack T. Ericson, of the Microfilming Corporation of America, who allowed me to work underfoot for a week while his staff was microfilming the papers of the American Association for Labor Legislation. The late Dr. Morris Fishbein graciously granted me an interview in May 1974 and later identified the probable authors of several *JAMA* editorials from the 1910s.

Judith W. Leavitt, Charles E. Rosenberg, Lloyd G. Stevenson, and Patricia Spain Ward each read a draft of this study and made numerous suggestions, some of which I pigheadedly ignored but all of which were excellent. Charlotte McGirr, Anne Millbrooke, and Susan Schultz aided at times with the tedious task of searching through old journals for scattered references to compulsory health insurance. Blanche Singer, of the University of Wisconsin Medical Library, processed more than my quota of interlibrary-loan requests. Kathryn Shain and Susan Duke typed the manuscript. William J. Orr, Jr., checked proofs, and Janet Koudelka once again proved the value of a first-rate editor.

Finally, my wife, Janet Schulze Numbers, helped in more ways than I can mention.

ALMOST PERSUADED

1. THE PROBLEM

...adequate medical service is available now only to the well-to-do who are able to pay and to the very poor who accept medical care as charity. The great body of middle class people cannot buy adequate medical service and will not ask for charity.

Ohio Health and Old Age Insurance Commission, 1919

America entered the second decade of the twentieth century experiencing rapid social and economic change. During the previous ten years its population had swelled over 20 percent to nearly 92,000,000, and by 1920 it would climb to over 105,000,000. For the first time in the country's history nearly half of the people lived in urban areas, where many of them were working over fifty hours a week as industrial laborers. Wages were rising, but so were prices; between 1912 and 1920 hourly earnings increased 130 percent, from 30 cents to 69 cents, while the general price index rose 93 percent.[1]

Medicine and public health were also changing at an unprecedented rate. The half century between 1870 and 1920, says Richard H. Shryock, produced "the most impressive record in all medical history."[2] The great plagues of the nineteenth century—smallpox, typhoid fever, diphtheria, typhus, malaria, cholera, and yellow fever—were either wiped out or being brought under control. Anesthesia and asepsis were revolutionizing surgery, and new diagnostic techniques like the x-ray were doing the same for the practice of medicine. Death rates were falling rapidly. For the cities of New York, Philadelphia, Boston, and New Orleans they dropped from 30.2 per 1,000 for the quarter century 1840-64 to 25.7 for 1865-89 and finally to 18.9 for 1890-1914.[3] The chief beneficiaries of this progress, however, were children. Adult death rates improved little if any.[4]

The extent of sickness among Americans in the early twentieth century is difficult to assess. Few communities kept morbidity records, and much illness, as always, went untreated and unreported. Yet some evidence is available. In a pioneering sickness survey of Rochester, New York, made for the Metropolitan Life Insurance Company in September 1915, Lee K. Frankel and Louis I. Dublin canvassed 7,638 families representing 14 percent of the city's population. They found over 2½ percent of the working population sick and unable to work, with "the chief causes of disability"

1

being rheumatism (73 cases), tuberculosis of the lungs (37 cases), cerebral hemorrhage and paralysis (34 cases), and mental alienation or insanity (25 cases). In addition, they turned up "56 persons disabled by chronic headache and neurasthenia, and 29 cases of ulcers and other diseases of the stomach." Generalizing from these findings, the investigators concluded that "throughout the year at least 2,147 males [were] sick," resulting in an estimated annual wage loss of $1,288,000 for the city of Rochester alone.[5] A second survey in Trenton, New Jersey, revealed similar conditions.[6] Nationally, the U.S. Public Health Service estimated in 1916 that each of the country's 30,000,000 workers missed an average of nine days a year because of sickness, which cost them over $800,000,000 in lost wages.[7]

Among the most significant findings of the Rochester survey was that only 63 percent of the employees too sick to work were seeing a physician, while only 45.3 percent of those sick but able to work were under professional care.[8] One factor contributing to this situation was the relatively high cost of medical assistance. A 1918 Pennsylvania study showed that physicians' fees ranged "from fifty cents to $5.00 for an office visit, and from $1.00 to $3.00 for a house call," with hospital-ward beds costing from $10.00 to $14.00 a week. For workers supporting large families on $2.00 a day, such fees were often prohibitive.[9]

Because many of the sick could neither afford to take time off from their jobs nor consult a physician, they continued to work while treating themselves at home, a practice often costly to both the individual and society. The case of John Callahan, discovered in Philadelphia by the Pennsylvania Health Insurance Commission, was no doubt typical of many:

Mr. Callahan was a tailor, who had worked for a prominent Philadelphia firm for several years. He was the father of four small children. Living up to the level of his income, with small savings, he felt he could not afford to be sick. He contracted tuberculosis, due undoubtedly in part to the industrial conditions in which he worked. He denied that he was sick and dosed himself continually with a patent medicine, warranted to "cure all ills." Finally, after a bad hemorrhage, he gave up, and when examined he was diagnosed an advanced case of tuberculosis. The family, up to this time always self-supporting, became dependent upon charity. One of his former employers gave $1.00 as [a] matter of charity; the others gave nothing. The children were all young, and Mrs. Callahan could not leave them to go out to work. Two of them were found to be tubercular. Mr. Callahan was only thirty-eight, and the family had no resources for the long future that loomed ahead. He was sent to Mount Alto, where little hope is given for his recovery; and for the past three years the family has been

"The Three Fears"

The Greatest of These Will Be Banished by Universal Health Insurance

Fig. 1. "The Three Fears": unemployment, want in old age, ill health (*American Labor Legislation Review*, 1919, *9:* 48).

cared for entirely by private philanthropy, at an expense of many hundreds of dollars. The oldest child is now [in 1918] only eleven. Meantime the state supports Mr. Callahan in a public sanatorium.[10]

One survey showed that 21.7 percent of the sick were treating themselves exclusively with patent medicines and home remedies, and another revealed that more than 71 percent were supplementing their physicians' prescriptions with over-the-counter drugs, for which they spent about $5.00 a year. The average amount spent on patent medicines by all families surveyed was $3.57, over twice that spent on prescriptions.[11]

The prevalence of self-medication was not, of course, solely a reflection of high medical costs. It also stemmed from a spirit of medical self-reliance and perhaps, in some locales, from a scarcity of physicians. Many places, it is true, had too many doctors; Wellington, Texas, population 87, boasted five, and throughout the country there was one physician for every 568 persons. Abraham Flexner, comparing these figures with the German ratio of one physician for every 2,000 inhabitants, concluded in 1910 that there was a national surplus.[12] But a subsequent study made by the American Medical Association raised questions about the validity of Flexner's assertion. Several factors, it pointed out, made such comparisons invalid:

For one thing, the density of population in this country, outside of the large cities, is very much lower than in Europe, and the physician's time cannot be utilized as intensively, and secondly, the paying ability of the large part of population of this country is very much larger....It is also important to remember that the obstetrical work in Europe is largely done by midwives, while in this country medical attendance at childbirth is much more common.[13]

The AMA's detailed study did indeed reveal a much more complex picture than the simple overcrowding painted by Flexner. It showed, among other things, that "the largest congestion of physicians" was not in the populous Eastern states, as was commonly supposed, but in the sparsely inhabited states of the West, where doctors frequently had widely scattered practices. Similarly, it revealed that the greatest proportionate number of physicians was not in the nation's largest cities, but in the towns with populations between 2,500 and 10,000, where doctors also served "the surrounding rural communities."[14] In rural areas there was only one physician for every 991 persons, but the scarcity of country doctors was not as serious as it had been just a few years earlier. The recent advent of the automobile was greatly increasing the efficiency of rural practitioners and giving farmers easy access to urban medical care.[15]

In spite of the growing demand for professional medical care, created largely by the promise of scientific medicine, the ratio of physicians to patients had scarcely changed since 1850. According to census figures, it had been 1:569 in 1850, 1:585 in 1880, and 1:582 in 1910. While the nation's population had increased 138 percent between 1870 and 1910—and the number of lawyers had risen by 200 percent, clergymen by 205 percent, teachers by 396 percent, and dentists by 410 percent—the medical profession had grown by only 153 percent, making it the "only important profession which had failed to increase substantially in proportion to the population." Moreover, since shortly after the turn of the century the supply of new doctors had been declining markedly. Between 1903 and 1914 the number of medical schools had fallen by over 33 percent; medical students, by 37.5 percent; and graduates, by 40 percent.[16] If America did have too many physicians, the condition did not seem permanent.

Certainly there was little doubt that the country suffered from a shortage of *well-qualified* practitioners. Despite recent advances in medical education and the passage of licensing laws, many American doctors were still incompetent. As one prominent Illinois physician observed in 1917, there was in most states "a very large percentage of the medical profession of most meager scientific qualifications with hundreds and thousands void of even ordinary, fundamental education." It was largely these physicians, he noted, who treated the poor.[17] Many Americans were also patronizing sectarian practitioners, who were often less competent than the poorly trained regulars. Besides homeopaths and eclectics, whose credentials were perhaps as good as those of some allopaths, there was a host of other healers from which to choose: "osteopaths, chiropractors, naprapaths, spondylotherapaths, mechanotherapaths, neurotherapaths, electrotherapaths, hydrotherapaths, suggestive therapaths, psychotherapaths, naturotherapaths, irridologists, magnetic healers, religious healers, and many other varieties."[18]

As a result of both social change and medical progress, particularly in surgery, hospitals by the second decade of the century were assuming an importance in medical care unknown only a short time before. In 1873 J. M. Toner could find only 178 hospitals in the entire country; forty years later there were 5,000.[19] Throughout most of the nineteenth century these institutions existed almost exclusively for the poor and homeless. Respectable persons were treated at home, where even the most difficult surgery was performed "on kitchen tables or ironing boards stretched between tables." By the turn of the century, however, the hospital was serving the sick rather than the poor and "had emerged as the center of advanced medical practice and a primary instrument in the health care of all social classes."[20] Costs varied from place to place, but in Illinois in 1919 weekly rates — covering room, board, medical, and nursing service — were $12.00 to $31.50 for a single room, $12.00 to $24.50 for a two-bed ward, $10.00 to $21.00 for a three- or four-bed ward, and $10.00 to $17.50 (or less) for a ward with five or more beds.[21]

Equally vital in providing medical care were the dispensaries and hospital outpatient departments found in most American cities. Originally created in the late eighteenth century to dispense medicine to the "worthy poor," dispensaries had evolved by the early 1900s into complex institutions offering the services of specialists to ambulatory patients for a nominal fee or nothing at all. As the century progressed, dispensaries gradually gave way to outpatient departments, which continued to serve the urban poor unable to afford the fees of private physicians.[22]

High costs coupled with increased benefits encouraged a number of

American workers—perhaps as many as one-third—to take out some kind of insurance against sickness.[23] This was done most commonly through trade unions, commercial insurance companies, or fraternal orders, the last of which provided an estimated half to three-fourths of all health insurance.[24] For most of the fraternals—organized by nationality, religion, or rites —sickness insurance was secondary to life insurance and generally provided only a cash benefit of $5.00 to $10.00 a week for a maximum of thirteen weeks, beginning after two weeks of illness. Few provided medical care, and those that did generally contracted with a physician at the lowest possible price.[25] This type of contract practice often resulted in shoddy medical care and elicited the nearly universal condemnation of other physicians.

Trade unions, the next largest carriers of health insurance, sometimes offered similar coverage. In California, for example, 41 percent of labor union members in 1916 were eligible for cash benefits when ill but, like members of fraternal orders, were seldom entitled to medical attendance.[26] Only a relative handful of American workers purchased health insurance policies from commercial insurance companies, and what they got was often far from satisfactory. According to one report, many of these companies insured only against rare diseases and included so many "technical clauses modifying the agreement . . . that apparently more is promised than paid."[27] Overall their significance was minimal.

In addition to these individually purchased plans, covering only what I. M. Rubinow called "the aristocracy of the working class,"[28] there were sickness benefit funds established by the more progressive industrial and business firms, particularly mining and lumber companies, and by many public utilities, like railroads.[29] These funds usually provided much better protection against sickness than those of fraternals and trade unions, and more frequently included medical care. Employees of the Milwaukee Electric Railway and Light Company, for example, received all necessary medical and surgical care for themselves and their dependents, plus $1.00 a day when unable to work. For this they paid 50 cents a month into an insurance fund, a sum matched by the company.[30] But such plans were not common, and they tended to "exist only among progressive employers where health hazards are often reduced to the minimum."[31]

Federal, state, and local government agencies had also long provided medical care for various segments of the American population, usually in the form of direct assistance rather than insurance.[32] Soon after the founding of the Republic, Congress passed a law establishing a health care system for merchant seamen, financed by a 20 cents a month tax on wages. The 1798 law authorized the President to use the funds thus collected "to provide for the temporary relief and maintenance of sick or disabled seamen, in the hospitals or other proper institutions now established in the several ports of the United States, or, in ports where no such institutions exist, then in such other manner as he shall direct: *Provided,* That the monies collected in any one district, shall be expended within the same." By 1872 thirty-two marine hospitals had been created, but the system ended twelve years later when American shipping interests complained that the added financial burden prevented them from competing successfully with English vessels.[33] The federal government also at times provided medical care for members of the armed forces, for veterans, for federal prisoners, for freed slaves, and, after the turn of the century, for Indians on reservations.[34]

Although the colony of Virginia established a mental asylum in 1773, significant state involvement with health care did not begin until the 1820s and 1830s with the building of public hospitals for the insane. By the close of the nineteenth century many states had also founded tuberculosis sanitoriums, as well as special hospitals for alcoholics, drug addicts, and epileptics.[35] But the boldest and most far-reaching state venture into health care, especially in terms of providing a model for compulsory health insurance, was the state university health service. About 1906 the University of California, for example, opened an infirmary where students, for a compulsory fee of $3.00 per semester, received complete medical, hospital, and nursing care. Local physicians protested and accused university doctors of unprofessional conduct in resorting to contract practice, but the successful experiments at Berkeley and on other campuses convinced many of the benefits of compulsory health insurance.[36]

The greatest government involvement in health matters came at the local level, although a 1912 survey revealed that no American city was making a systematic effort "to provide really effective medical care for the sick poor."[37] Since the seventeenth century, American towns, following Elizabethan poor law, had commonly assumed responsibility for their sick poor, housing them in almshouses and contracting with local practitioners to provide medical attendance.[38] During the nineteenth century, particularly in the latter half, a number of cities and counties built hospitals where the poor could receive free care, and many communities operated isolation hospitals—"pest houses"—for patients suffering from contagious diseases.

In some cities, especially in New York, local governments subsidized dispensaries or free clinics, which for many citizens represented "the only alternative to purchase by private contract in the field of medical service."[39]

As more and more workers, unable to afford private physicians but otherwise self-sufficient, turned to dispensaries, the medical profession grew increasingly suspicious that these institutions were treating patients fully capable of paying. Investigations in New York, Boston, St. Louis, and other cities, however, showed "that only a small percentage, from two to five, of dispensary patients are really able to pay for the medical service they seek to obtain free or upon payment of a nominal fee."[40] A New York survey, conducted in 1912 for the Medical Society of the County of New York, concluded that "the general run of patients who visit dispensaries are worthy of free treatment." Only 10 percent of dispensary patients seemed able to pay for medical treatment "under ordinary circumstances," but their financial condition was usually so precarious that "in illness demanding continued treatment or the services of a specialist, to pay a physician would mean for them serious deprivation or the incurring of debt from which afterwards it would be difficult to escape."[41]

By the 1910s some city health departments, created originally to provide sanitation and prevent disease, were, as one critic saw it, passing "beyond the confines of preventive medicine—to the practice of medicine."[42] In New York City the Board of Health not only administered certain vaccines and anti-toxins, like that given to rabies victims, but operated an expanding school health program. At first limited merely to examining children with health problems, the program by 1914 was operating a number of clinics that not only diagnosed but treated. This was justified on the grounds, as Lillian D. Wald put it, "that it was foolish to examine children without seeing that they received treatment." When Dr. S. S. Goldwater took over as health commissioner in 1914, he could see no reason why medical attention should terminate with the child. Consequently, he established an experimental health district on the lower east side of Manhattan with a staff of one physician and three nurses to serve a twenty-block area inhabited by about 25,000 persons. The experiment worked so well that Goldwater's successor, Haven Emerson, set up four additional health districts, and other cities were soon imitating New York.[43]

Needless to say, some private practitioners viewed these developments with apprehension. One group of physicians pointedly accused the New York City Health Department of following "a policy of Socialism" and described its programs as "ruinous to the business of the medical practitioners of the city." It seems, as John Duffy says, that "as long as the department's medical inspectors merely reported thousands of physical defects among school children, the medical profession had no objection, but the opening of clinics to correct these conditions was another story."[44]

In view of the government's expanding role in providing medical care, the overcrowding of the profession in some areas, and the competition from irregular practitioners, American physicians grew increasingly concerned about their financial status. Medical journals across the country bemoaned the low income of doctors, which they sometimes estimated to be as low as $500 or $750 a year, scarcely more than that earned by manual laborers.[45] In 1913 the Judicial Council of the American Medical Association reported "that hardly more than 10 per cent of the physicians in the United States are able to earn a comfortable income."[46] Two years later the *New York State Journal of Medicine* observed that "50 per cent of the general practitioners of New York City at present find it difficult to meet their current expenses, economize as they will."[47] Only surgeons and some other specialists seemed to be benefitting from the country's economic prosperity.[48]

Aside from these frequent laments, the little available evidence suggests that the medical profession was probably not as badly off as it imagined. A survey of 330 physicians and surgeons in Richmond, Virginia (apparently in 1915), showed that although "the very large proportion of physicians were earning less than $2,000," thirty-two had annual incomes over $4,000 and five of these—four surgeons and an unidentified specialist—made over $5,000. One of the surgeons earned $42,000; another, $23,000; but part of their income may have been from nonmedical sources.[49] Income tax records for Wisconsin in 1914 indicate that although less than 60 percent of the state's more than 2,800 physicians paid taxes, the average income of the taxed physicians was $1,488. This figure compared with $3,581 for bankers and capitalists, $2,810 for manufacturers, $2,568 for lawyers, $648 for professors, and $976 for other professions.[50] The restlessness of American physicians—for the years 1910 through 1914 the number of experienced physicians sitting for state board examinations was 58 percent higher than the number of recent medical school graduates[51]—suggests that many were having a hard time financially, but it might just as well be a manifestation of the universal desire to seek greener pastures.

If any physicians were suffering financially, they were the independent general practitioners, whose incomes were apparently not even keeping up with rising costs.[52] One reason for this was that they were losing their patients: the rich to specialists, the contagious to public health doctors, and the poor to dispensaries and hospital outpatient departments.[53] Although there was still little of what was called "organized" or group practice,[54] and although general practitioners continued to provide the bulk of American medical services, "the old-time relation between the doctor and the family, and especially the wage-earning family," seemed to be fast disappearing.[55]

From the patient's point of view, especially the wage-earner's, the situation was just as bleak. For the first time in history the value of medicine was indisputable; yet rising costs were tending to limit adequate care "to the well-to-do who are able to pay and to the very poor who accept medical care as charity." As one investigative commission observed, "The great body of middle class people cannot buy adequate medical service and will not ask for charity."[56] Faced with similar conditions, many European countries had recently adopted some form of compulsory health insurance.[57] Beginning with Germany, which passed legislation in 1883, the movement spread rapidly to Austria (1888), Hungary (1891), Luxembourg (1901), Norway (1909), Serbia (1910), Great Britain (1911), Russia (1912), Roumania (1912), and the Netherlands (1913).[58] "From the frozen shores of Norway down to the sunny clime of Italy, from the furthest East and up to Spain, all Europe, whether Germanic, Saxon, Latin, or Slav," was following the same path, wrote I. M. Rubinow.[59] In terms of influence on America, the most important of the European plans were the German and the British.

Chancellor Otto von Bismarck created the German system of social insurance as a dike to hold back the rising tide of socialism. As he told a visiting British observer, he wanted "to bribe the working classes, or, if you like, to win them over to regard the State as a social institution existing for their sake and interested in their welfare."[60] In 1883 he succeeded in winning Reichstag approval, and sickness insurance went into effect on December 1, 1884. The original act, which limited coverage to certain categories of workers, was amended from time to time to include "practically all industry, building, mines, quarries, transportation, commerce, and certain office employees." Finally, in 1911, an Insurance Consolidation Act brought virtually all employees under the plan, including agricultural and domestic workers, teachers, actors, and musicians, "regardless of the artistic value of their performances."

Although insurance was compulsory for all workers, regardless of their wages, supervisory personnel, like foremen and ship captains, were liable only if their annual incomes did not exceed 2,500 marks. Others earning less than that amount could enroll voluntarily. All told, the system embraced about 31 percent of the total population and about 77 percent of all persons gainfully employed.

Insurance benefits included medical care, medicines, and other necessary items like eye glasses and trusses. In addition, beginning with their fourth day of illness and continuing for a maximum of twenty-six weeks (when invalidity insurance took over), members received sick pay equal to half of their wages. When appropriate, hospitalization was available in lieu of medical care and sick pay. Women members were eligible for an eight-week maternity benefit equal to sick pay, and coverage could be extended to the families of members if supplementary contributions were made. Finally, there was a funeral benefit to ensure workers a decent burial.

Employees and employers jointly bore the cost of this plan, with the former paying two-thirds and the latter one-third of the premium. These contributions went into local mutual funds, *Krankenkassen,* organized by factory, occupation, or geographical area. The largest of these funds, the Leipzig Federation of Sickness Funds, had a membership in 1910 of 182,898, embracing the entire city and its suburbs lying within a four-mile radius. Committees of employees and employers, composed of two workers for every representative from management, administered the funds, under the general supervision of state-run insurance offices.

The most common sources of friction between the sickness funds and physicians concerned payment and freedom of choice. Depending on the fund involved, physicians could be paid either by case according to official fee schedules or by capitation, and negotiations over these issues were often strained. Conflict also arose over physicians' demands for panels open to all private practitioners, from which patients were free to choose their doctor.

The architect of the British health insurance system, David Lloyd George, visited Germany in 1908 and returned brimming with enthusiasm for its system of social insurance.[61] Motivated primarily by a desire to raise the British standard of living, he prodded Parliament in 1911 to pass a National Insurance Act, effective January 15, 1913, which, with few exceptions, made health insurance mandatory for all employed persons between the ages of sixteen and seventy.

Following passage of the bill, an apprehensive British Medical Association presented Lloyd George with a list of six demands, the famous "Six Cardinal Points." In brief they were: (1) an income limit of two pounds a week for the insured, (2) free choice of physician by the patient, (3) administration of the medical benefit by local health committees composed of doctors, (4) method of payment to be decided by a vote of district physicians, (5) adequate remuneration, generally taken to be 8s. 6d. per patient, and (6) adequate medical representation on all administrative bodies. Eventually the government agreed to all but two of the demands, refusing to set an income limit below three pounds and to pay a capitation fee above 6s. 6d.

British Workman's Social Insurance Protection Compared with American Workman's

Which umbrella would you *prefer on the inevitable "rainy day"?*

Fig. 2. From *American Labor Legislation Review,* 1910, *9:* 65.

(7s. for tuberculosis patients), which was considerably more than many physicians had been making. By January 15 the majority of general practitioners, attracted by the prospect of higher incomes and intimidated by the chancellor's veiled threat to put them all on salary if resistance continued, had signed on with the program and were ready to work.

The National Insurance Act provided five kinds of benefits: (1) a medical benefit entitling the insured to free medicines, approved appliances, and the attendance of a panel general practitioner, the size of whose practice was unlimited; (2) a sanatorial benefit for those with tuberculosis; (3) a sickness benefit of 10s. a week per man and 7s. 6d. a week per woman, beginning on the fourth day of illness and continuing for up to twenty-six weeks; (4) a disability benefit, which continued the sickness benefit at a rate of 5s. a week for the duration of the illness; and (5) a maternity benefit of one and a half pounds. Unlike the German plan, the British act did not provide for hospitalization or specialist care.

For this insurance the British worker paid only 4d. a week or 44 1/2 percent of the total cost, compared with the 66 2/3 percent paid by German employees. (Women paid even less: 3d. a week or 37 1/2 percent of the cost.) The employer and the state split the remaining contribution, with the former paying 3d. and the state, 2d. These premiums did not go to designated mutual funds, as in Germany, but to the friendly society[62] of the worker's choice, which contracted with physicians for their services. These societies, similar to the American fraternals, had long provided medical assistance, and they now operated under the supervision of a government commission, which employed "a bewildering complex system of bookkeeping [to control] the income and outgo of every 'approved' society, the transfers of member-ship, and the resulting movements of reserve values, etc."[63]

In 1912, when the American campaign for compulsory health insurance began, it was still too early to tell with certainty what effects the European experiments were having on public health and the profession of medicine. But early reports were generally positive, and reformers were optimistic that compulsory health insurance would go a long way toward solving the problem of inadequate medical care for American workers.

2. THE REFORMERS

[Compulsory health insurance] is not a panacea. It will not bring the millenium. But there is no other measure now before the public which equals the power of health insurance toward social regeneration.

> *Irving Fisher,*
> *President of the American Association for Labor Legislation,*
> *to the Medical Society of the County of New York, January, 1917*

The American health-insurance debate was a product of early-twentieth-century Progressivism. This multi-faceted attempt to reform American society gave rise to a wide spectrum of activities, ranging from trust-busting to crusades for social justice. Socially minded Progressives hoped to eradicate the evils of the old economic order primarily by means of labor legislation. Their agenda for reform included abolishing child labor, setting maximum hours and minimum wages for women workers, and providing insurance against industrial accidents, unemployment, old age, and sickness.[1]

Such reforms, of course, necessitated a revision of traditional American political philosophy. As Sidney Fine has shown, there was already by the turn of the century a noticeable drift away from laissez faire in the direction of a general-welfare state, as various governmental agencies assumed greater responsibilities in health, education, and welfare. But much remained to be done, and the social Progressives intended to do it by striking a happy balance between "the known evils of laissez faire and the anticipated evils of socialism."[2] The sponsors of social insurance, having repudiated the "old individualism," now appealed to the state to assume responsibilities previously in private hands. "Our conception of the function of the State is changing," said one insurance advocate. "The well-being or ill-being of the individual is now looked upon as a social asset or liability and not simply as a matter of personal concern alone to the individual."[3]

Prior to the passage of the British National Insurance Act in 1911 few Americans displayed any interest in social insurance. The United States Commissioner of Labor had published John Graham Brooks' study of the German system in 1893 and William F. Willoughby's more comprehensive report on European social insurance in 1898, but these publications attracted little attention. Likewise, the Socialist Party's call for sickness insurance in 1904, the first endorsement by an American political organization, scarcely

Fig. 3. John B. Andrews (Irving Fisher and Eugene L. Fisk, *How to Live,* New York: Funk & Wagnalls, 1915).

stirred the public's interest. Much more significant was the plank on health insurance adopted by Theodore Roosevelt's Progressive Party in 1912. This called for "The protection of home life against hazards of sickness, irregular employment and old age through the adoption of a system of social insurance adapted to American use."[4]

The major credit for raising the issue of health insurance in the United States belongs to the American Association for Labor Legislation (AALL), a branch of the International Association for Labor Legislation and one of "the most influential of the social Progressive societies."[5] This body, founded in 1906 by a group of reform-minded social scientists eager to translate the principles of social justice into concrete legislation, had close academic ties. Among its earliest presidents were such prominent academicians as Richard T. Ely of Wisconsin, Henry W. Farnam and Irving Fisher of Yale, Henry Seager and Samuel McCune Lindsay of Columbia, and Willoughby of Princeton. The Wisconsin labor economist John R. Commons served as secretary from 1908 to 1909, when he arranged to turn his duties over to his former student John B. Andrews, who had been assisting him for the past year or so. By 1913 the energetic young Andrews had succeeded in

Fig. 4. Frederick L. Hoffman (S. Adolphus
Knopf, *A History of the National Tuberculosis
Association,* New York City, National Tubercu-
losis Association, 1922).

raising membership from a few hundred to over 3,000 and had emerged
as the most powerful figure in the association.[6]

The AALL's earliest reform efforts focused on securing legislation to
compensate workers for industrial accidents and to combat industrial
diseases. Their most notable success came in 1912 with the passage of a
federal law prohibiting the match industry from using poisonous phospho-
rus. When absorbed, this substance produced a loathsome condition known
as "phossy jaw," which often resulted in loss of teeth and decomposition of
jaw bones. In campaigning against this disease, the AALL pursued a three-
phase program of investigation, education, and legislation—an approach it
would later use with effect in advocating compulsory health insurance. This
strategy paid off in the spring of 1912, when Congress approved the AALL-
sponsored bill by an overwhelming majority and President William Howard
Taft signed it into law. This victory, claims one historian, "catapulted the
Association into a position of leadership in the movement for protective
labor legislation and social insurance" and focused national attention on the
subject of industrial illness.[7]

Flushed with victory, the self-confident AALL leaders next turned their
attention to social insurance for industrial workers. At its annual meeting in
Boston in December 1912, the Association voted to create a Committee on
Social Insurance "to study conditions impartially, to investigate the operation
of existing systems of insurance, to prepare carefully for needed legislation,
and to stimulate intelligent discussion."[8] In January President Willoughby,

a pioneer investigator himself, nominated the following committee members: Edward T. Devine (chairman), Henry R. Seager, Miles M. Dawson, Frederick L. Hoffman, Charles R. Henderson, Henry J. Harris, John Koren (soon replaced by Carroll W. Doten), and Isaac M. Rubinow. Andrews served as secretary.[9]

These men, Hoffman noted approvingly, formed "an excellent working crowd," since the members all knew one another and worked well together.[10] Indeed, the committee was outstanding. The chairman, Devine, was director of the New York School of Philanthropy and one of the nation's best-known social workers. Seager was an economics professor at Columbia University, a former president of the AALL, and author of a book on social insurance in Europe. Dawson was a consulting actuary in New York and co-author (with Lee K. Frankel) of a recent study of *Workingmen's Insurance in Europe.* Hoffman, a statistician with the Prudential Life Insurance Company, was perhaps the country's foremost authority on industrial diseases. Henderson was a sociologist at the University of Chicago; Harris served as chief of the Division of Documents at the Library of Congress; and Koren and Doten represented the American Statistical Association.

The only physician on the committee and the only one publicly committed to compulsory health insurance was Rubinow,[11] a member of the Socialist Party who had not practiced medicine for ten years. Following his arrival in the United States from Russia in 1893, he had obtained an M.D. degree from the Medical College of New York University, practiced for

Fig. 5. Isaac M. Rubinow ("The Social Front of Twenty-five Years," *Survey Midmonthly,* May 1938, *74:* 148).

five years among New York's poor, and finally abandoned medicine for statistics and the social sciences. A seminar with E. R. A. Seligman at Columbia University aroused his interest in social insurance, and in 1911, as a result of work done for the U.S. Bureau of Labor Statistics, he prepared a comparative study of workmen's insurance in Italy, Russia, and Spain, which doubled as a doctoral dissertation in political science. Two years later he published an influential volume on *Social Insurance, with Special Reference to American Conditions,* the outgrowth of a series of lectures given the previous spring at the New York School of Philanthropy. At the time of his appointment to the Committee on Social Insurance he was without question the best-informed person on health insurance in the United States.[12]

The committee's initial undertaking was educational: organizing the first nationwide conference on social insurance, which its sponsors optimistically hoped would be "the precursor of a great awakening in the United States to the importance of the subject." About a hundred persons gathered in Chicago in June 1913 and listened to papers on all varieties of social insurance, including one on sickness insurance by Rubinow. The response, however, was disappointing. His remarks elicited "scant" discussion, but Rubinow consoled himself with the knowledge that "as yet little thought has been given in this country to the insurance method of meeting these problems." Less understandable was the opposition of his fellow committeeman Hoffman, who argued that the expansion of voluntary plans would eliminate the need for compulsion.[13]

Hoffman, already emerging as the most outspoken American critic of compulsory health insurance, was a largely self-educated German immigrant who through dedication and intelligence had worked his way up from grocery clerk to statistician of the Prudential. His studies of Negro morbidity and mortality and his statistical analyses of industrial health hazards, particularly his investigation of tuberculosis in the dusty trades, won him a reputation for unimpeachable scholarship. The editor of the *Pennsylvania Medical Journal* referred to him as "the most reliable statistician in America (if not in the world),"[14] and a president of the American Medical Association referred to his statistics as being "never questioned."[15] In 1911 Hoffman was elected president of the American Statistical Association. His connection with the AALL began in 1909, when he helped to organize a New Jersey branch of the Association. His subsequent efforts in the anti-phosphorous match campaign resulted in appointment to the AALL's twelve-man executive committee; and at the time of his nomination to the Committee on Social Insurance, he was also serving as chairman of the Industrial Hygiene

Committee. In social and political matters, he was resolutely conservative, "a vigorous exponent of private enterprise, a staunch advocate of Anglo-Saxon racial purity, and a zealous guardian of the traditional elements of American society and life."[16]

Although the Social Insurance Committee's assignment embraced all forms of social insurance—accident, unemployment, old age, and sickness—the members decided to concentrate first on health insurance, which they considered to be the most urgently needed. The rationale for this decision was simple: the committee's principal objective was the reduction of destitution and demoralization in American society, and sickness was one of the greatest causes of poverty.[17] A 1909 study of 31,481 charity cases by the United States Immigration Commission revealed that sickness was six and a half times more likely to cause dependency than an industrial accident; and a report of the Charity Organization Society in Buffalo, New York, had recently concluded that sickness "far exceeds unemployment as a cause of poverty."

As Robert Bremner has shown, "confidence in the eradicability of poverty" was a major stimulus to Progressive reform. Life in an increasingly urban and industrial society had undermined the old nineteenth-century belief that an individual failed because of "some weakness or defect in his own character." By the turn of the century "there was a wide-spread conviction that the causes of failure were to be found, in most cases, in circumstances outside and beyond the control of individual personality." Thus the social Progressives sought to cure poverty primarily by correcting "unjust and degrading conditions of work and living."[18]

As the 1915 survey of Rochester, New York, had so amply documented, sickness was particularly evident among American wage-earners. In fact, a considerable part of this excessive morbidity seemed to be directly attributable to industrial conditions. Tuberculosis—the "captain of death"—was the leading cause of mortality in 96 of 140 occupations in the United States and was especially prevalent in dusty trades like sand blasting, stone cutting, and mining. Industrial workers also suffered from more than their share of degenerative diseases affecting the heart, vascular system, and kidneys. Because the incidence of these ailments had practically doubled since 1885, the committee was convinced that they were, "in part, a result of the industrial strain imposed upon men." Finally, several studies had shown that infant mortality was unusually high in the families of wage-earners, many of whom could not afford proper medical care.

The plight of the working class, as the committee saw it, was further compounded by the expense of modern medicine, which was often beyond the means of manual laborers. Recent advances in medicine, especially in the area of laboratory, x-ray, and surgical services, had facilitated diagnosis and treatment, but they had also driven up costs. Free dispensaries and hospital wards helped some, but they were insufficient and tended to destroy the self-respect of those who used them. Only a small percentage of industrial workers carried voluntary sickness insurance, and those who needed it the most—the lowest paid—seldom had it.

The Committee on Social Insurance saw compulsory sickness insurance as part of a larger campaign for the conservation of health that paralleled the popular movement for the conservation of natural resources. Thus its members emphasized prevention as much as cures. By providing medical care, compulsory health insurance would assist in catching diseases in their early stages and preventing disability; and by placing a cash value on illness, it would stimulate preventive measures like factory sanitation and periodic physical examinations.

To facilitate the preparation of a model insurance bill, the committee appointed a subcommittee apparently consisting of Seager, Rubinow, and Joseph P. Chamberlain, a lawyer with the Columbia University Legislative Drafting Research Fund.[19] By the summer of 1914 these men had reached agreement on nine basic standards to be incorporated into any proposed bill:

1. To be effective health insurance should be compulsory, on the basis of joint contributions of employer, employee and the state.
2. The compulsory insurance should include all wage workers earning less than a given annual sum, where employed with sufficient regularity to make it practicable to compute and collect assessments. Casual and home workers should, as far as practicable, be included within the plan and scope of a compulsory system.
3. There should be a voluntary supplementary system for groups of persons (wage workers or others) who for practical reasons are kept out of the compulsory system.
4. Health insurance should provide for a specified period only, provisionally set at twenty-six weeks (one-half year), but a system of invalidity insurance should be combined with health insurance so that all disability due to disease will be taken care of in one law, although the funds should be separate.
5. Health insurance on the compulsory plan should be carried by mutual local funds jointly managed by employers and employees under public supervision . . . .
6. Invalidity insurance should be carried by funds covering a larger geographical

area comprising the districts of a number of local health insurance funds . . . .
7. Both health and invalidity insurance should include medical service, supplies, necessary nursing and hospital care . . . .
8. Cash benefits should be provided by both invalidity and health insurance for the insured or his dependents during such disability.
9. It is highly desirable that prevention be emphasized . . . . [20]

The subcommittee anticipated trouble in winning unanimous approval for their standards, and their fears were not unfounded. Opposition came primarily from the two members with insurance connections, Dawson and Hoffman, who objected to the exclusion of commercial companies as carriers. The subcommittee, "with some little difficulty," eventually converted Dawson, but Hoffman remained skeptical. Although he claimed that he would not oppose compulsory health insurance if the need for it could be "as clearly and concisely established as was the case in workmen's compensation legislation," his main objection seemed to be the committee's unwillingness to utilize existing insurance carriers. Chamberlain, for one, was sure that Hoffman's views were not unrelated to his ties with the Prudential.[21]

While the Committee on Social Insurance proceeded to hammer out a model bill, AALL staffers were conducting various investigations. The most important of these concerned the operation of compulsory health insurance in Europe, the success or failure of which was to become a major debating point. As the United States became more urban and industrialized, differences between the Old and New Worlds rapidly disappeared. American reformers, with little in their own past to guide them, thus looked with increasing frequency "to an older Europe as a laboratory which had developed methods to solve such problems."[22] As early as January 1914 Chamberlain wrote Andrews suggesting that he obtain preliminary information from his contacts in Germany, England, Switzerland, and Norway. Specifically, he sought answers to three questions: (1) Were medical benefits being satisfactorily administered? (2) Had health insurance reduced the incomes of doctors in working-class communities? (3) Were physicians, especially those in Great Britain, making more money under the National Insurance Act than they had previously received from the friendly societies? "We need to know what was done, why it succeeded, or did not succeed, that we may pattern after success and avoid disaster," he explained.[23]

By the summer of 1914 the committee had reached the point where it needed "exact information" regarding the European situation and suggested that Katharine Coman, a Wellesley College economist who had been observing social insurance in Europe, be asked to provide it. Although the members were already committed to the German system of local mutuals, endorsed in the nine standards, they wanted an exhaustive comparison of this plan with the British system of approved societies before submitting a model bill. Unfortunately, Coman had already returned from England, but, when contacted, she recommended her "young friend and collaborator," Olga S. Halsey, as a substitute. Halsey was then in London studying the National Insurance Act and planned to visit the Continent during the summer. She accepted the invitation to become a special investigator for the AALL and shortly thereafter issued a report on the British system that confirmed the committee's suspicions.[24]

Following "a lively debate" at the AALL's annual meeting in December, the delegates voted to endorse the Social Insurance Committee's nine standards for a model bill, a rough draft of which was already being circulated.[25] Apparently some of the more eager members wanted to introduce the bill immediately, but Hoffman, at least, was adamantly opposed. "I seriously question the introduction of an ill-digested, ill-considered *health insurance bill,* even in a single State Legislature at the present time," he wrote Andrews. Existing voluntary plans still seemed adequate to him, and, besides, he feared that the committee's proposal was not "in conformity to our American methods of government."[26] By this time the Prudential statistician was publicly criticizing the Committee on Social Insurance for its contrived and un-American "propaganda."[27]

Since Hoffman refused even to allow his name to be used in connection with the tentative draft, Chamberlain began to despair of ever obtaining unanimous approval for the bill he was preparing. The immediate problem was solved, however, on April 10, 1916, when Hoffman resigned in disgust.[28] Gone but not forgotten, he continued to haunt the committee's efforts for the duration of the debate.

Whatever dampening effect Hoffman's departure may have had was more than offset in October 1915 by the addition of three new members: Alexander Lambert, S. S. Goldwater, and Lillian D. Wald.[29] Over a year earlier Katharine Coman had recommended greater cooperation with the medical profession in order to avoid the difficulties that had arisen in Great Britain. It would be a great advantage, she thought, to capture "this stronghold in the outset of the campaign."[30] Andrews, however, was dubious about

Fig. 6. Alexander Lambert (*JAMA*, 1919, *72:* facing p. 1652).

such prospects. While conceding that medical support "might head off much opposition," he feared that most doctors "are not exactly what we would call social minded."[31] The new appointees were definitely socially minded, but hardly typical physicians. Both Lambert and Goldwater were "institution men and medical employers" and thus, according to one New York practitioner, were unqualified to "speak for the rank and file of the profession" on the subject of health insurance.[32]

Alexander Lambert came from a prominent New York medical family and was nationally known as one of former President Roosevelt's hunting and fishing companions. A graduate of Yale University and the College of Physicians and Surgeons of Columbia University, he had spent two years in the early 1890s continuing his medical studies in Europe. In addition to a large private practice (that included the Roosevelt family), he served as attending physician at Bellevue Hospital and as Clinical Professor of Medicine at Cornell University Medical College. At the time of his appointment to the Committee on Social Insurance he was chairman of the AMA's Judicial Council, a highly visible post in organized medicine.[33]

S. S. Goldwater was scarcely less prominent than Lambert, but his background was more like Rubinow's. The son of a Jewish tobacconist

Fig. 7. S. S. Goldwater (Irving Fisher and
Eugene L. Fisk, *How to Live,* New York:
Funk & Wagnalls, 1915).

and pharmacist, he dropped out of school at the age of thirteen and four
years later became editor of a New York garment-trades journal. This
experience awakened his interest in social problems and led to his return to
school. After a year studying political science at Columbia University and a
second year at the University of Leipzig, he enrolled in the Medical College
of New York University, just three years behind Rubinow. His intention was
to use medicine as "a stepping stone" to a career in public health, which is
precisely what he did. Upon graduation in 1901, he became assistant
superintendent of the Mount Sinai Hospital, where he pioneered in the
development of social services. In 1908 he served as president of the
American Hospital Association, and the two years prior to his joining the
Committee on Social Insurance were spent as commissioner of health for
New York City.[34]

The third new appointee, Lillian Wald, represented still another branch
of medicine: public health nursing. A graduate of the New York Hospital
school for nurses in 1891, she briefly attended the Women's Medical College
in New York City before quitting to organize home nursing services for the
city's poor. Her Nurses' Settlement on Henry Street became a model for
public health nursing programs, and she herself won fame as a reformer,

especially in the area of child labor. At the time of her appointment to the AALL committee, she was president of the National Organization for Public Health Nursing.[35]

One month after the addition of its three new members the Committee on Social Insurance published a tentative draft of its bill, deliberately omitting the specific role of the medical profession, which was to be worked out later in consultation with representative physicians. Demand for the draft far exceeded expectations. Within a few weeks the first run of 8,000 copies was exhausted, and a second edition of 5,000 was printed. Although the committee had patterned its bill more after the German than the English system, they decided to discontinue using the German term "sickness insurance" and adopt instead the more positive English expression "health insurance." This phrase, they explained, "calls attention to the main object of the act, the conservation of health, that is, the prevention and treatment of sickness, as well as provision of financial benefits." The committee also hoped to correct the common opinion that social insurance was a peculiarly German invention, a view growing increasingly unpopular since the outbreak of war in Europe.[36]

The model bill, which Andrews proudly described as a combination of "the best points of the British and the German systems,"[37] required the participation of virtually all manual laborers earning $100 a month or less. Government employees, already covered, were exempt, as were most domestic and casual workers. Self-employed persons with incomes under $100 a month could enroll on a voluntary basis.

Benefits were of four kinds: (1) Each insured worker—and each member of his family—was entitled to complete medical, surgical, and nursing care, plus all medical and surgical supplies. (2) Beginning with the fourth day of illness and continuing for a maximum of twenty-six weeks, members were eligible for cash benefits equal to two-thirds of their weekly wages. (Unlike the English plan, the bill made no provision for invalidity insurance covering disabilities lasting longer than a half year.) If hospitalized, a worker would receive one-third of his wages to support his family. (3) In case of pregnancy, insured women and the wives of insured men were entitled to all necessary medical, surgical, and obstetrical aid, and all materials and appliances. In addition, insured women were eligible for an eight-week maternity benefit equal to that allowed in times of illness. (4) All members were entitled to a maximum of $50 for funeral expenses.

Premiums were to be divided among the state, the employer, and the employee, with the state generally paying 20 percent, the employer 40 percent, and the employee 40 percent. The employer's percentage increased to 48 percent for workers earning between $8 and $9 a week, and went to 80 percent for employees making less than $5. The amount paid would depend on actual expenses, but the AALL estimated that the premium for a person earning $50 a month would be about $2, of which the worker would pay 80¢.

In selecting the most desirable means for providing insurance, the committee had three choices. The insurance could be carried "(1) by a state fund managed entirely by the state, as are workmen's compensation funds now existing in several states; (2) by approved societies, as in England; or (3) by district mutual associations, as in Germany." Fear of a mammoth bureaucracy and possible corruption ruled out a state fund; the English experience with approved societies eliminated that option; so the committee elected for local insurance societies, supervised by a state social insurance commission and governed locally by an equal number of employer and employee representatives. This was "practically the German plan," with one major difference: in Germany two-thirds of the directors were employees.

With model bill in hand and an apparently receptive public, John Andrews looked forward late in 1915 to "a big educational campaign for the conservation of health," with "fair prospects" for the establishment of health insurance commissions to investigate the topic in 1916 and for the actual passage of legislation the year following.[38] In hopes of enlisting the support of organized medicine in this campaign, in mid-November he sent a copy of the tentative draft to Dr. Frederick R. Green, secretary of the AMA's Council on Health and Public Instruction.[39]

3. THE PHYSICIANS

Your plans [for compulsory health insurance] are so entirely in line with our own that I want to be of every possible assistance.
  Dr. Frederick R. Green,
  Secretary of the AMA Council on Health and Public Instruction,
  to John B. Andrews, Secretary of the AALL, November 1915

The American Medical Association and its constituent state and local societies represented in 1915 little more than half of all physicians in the United States.[1] Yet for the first time in its history the AMA was the undisputed leader of American medicine. Throughout the nineteenth century it had been weak and ineffectual. Founded in 1847 by a small group of regular physicians concerned about the low quality of medical education and the encroachment of sectarian practitioners, it had never fulfilled its early promise. During its first fifty years it had devoted most of its limited energies to questions of medical practice, largely ignoring social issues and seldom venturing into the political arena. On occasion it had lobbied for vital statistics and public health legislation, but President Charles A. L. Reed noted sadly in 1901 that it had "exerted relatively little influence on legislation, either state or national." At this time only about 7 percent of the country's physicians were members.[2]

A large part of the AMA's ineffectiveness was the result of internal quarreling and poor organization. The original constitution had established three types of membership. First, there were the annually elected *delegates* representing "permanently organized societies, medical colleges, hospitals, lunatic asylums and other permanently organized medical institutions of good standing," that is, those which subscribed to the Association's Code of Ethics. Each state and local medical society was entitled to one delegate for every ten regular resident members; nonsectarian medical colleges and hospitals with over a hundred inmates were allowed two; and "other" institutions could send one. A second category consisted of *members by invitation* and accommodated interested physicians from regions of the country not represented by delegates from established institutions and societies. Third, there were the nonvoting *permanent members,* generally former delegates but also including a few physicians elected by unanimous vote. In the mid-1870s the AMA decided to eliminate most of the delegate positions not representing approved medical societies, but many delegates still represented societies with few AMA members. To compound the problem of organization, the number of delegates was getting out of hand. If all eligible societies had sent their full quotas of delegates, attendance at general meetings would have topped 2,000.[3]

The absence of an adequate staff and permanent headquarters also retarded the growth of the AMA. Except for the office of permanent secretary, created in 1864, all offices were held for only one year. No board of trustees existed until 1882, and the home office in Chicago was not purchased until after the turn of the century.[4]

By 1900 the situation was clearly intolerable, and at the annual session that year a three-man committee was appointed to diagnose the problem and prescribe a solution. The committee, after a year's deliberation, recommended a complete reorganization. They proposed to weld local, state, and national units into one representative society that would "foster scientific medicine and . . . make the medical profession a power in the social and political life of the republic." Henceforth, membership in a local (generally county) society would automatically carry membership in the state and national organizations. To replace the unwieldy general meetings, the committee recommended the creation of a new legislative body, the House of Delegates, whose members would be elected by the state legislative bodies, which in turn would be elected by the county societies. Each state or territorial society would be entitled to one delegate for every 500 members, so long as the total number of delegates never exceeded 150. The three government services — Army, Navy, and Marine-Hospital — and each of the AMA's scientific sections, created from time to time in response to the pressures of medical specialization, were also allowed one delegate.[5]

This plan, approved at the 1901 annual session, produced immediate results. Most state societies fell into line quickly, and membership in the AMA increased over seven-fold within five years. Under the new system, the board of trustees and executive officers carried out the will of the House of Delegates, which met annually as a legislative body.

Along with reorganization, the AMA in 1902 established permanent headquarters in Chicago and began its bureaucratic growth. Within a few years several standing committees or councils, each with its own full-time secretary, had come into existence. In 1873 a Judicial Council had been created to rule on legal and ethical questions. This was joined in 1904 by a Council on Medical Education, in 1905 by a Council on Pharmacy and Chemistry, and in 1910 by a Council on Health and Public Instruction, the object of which was to develop "public confidence in the purposes and work of the American Medical Association and of the profession."

The reorganization and growth of the AMA infused it with new life. Traditionally conservative,[6] the Association shortly after 1900 entered a brief period of reform, lobbying for pure food and drug legislation, a national health department, and the extension of public health laws. To upgrade medical education, it requested state subsidies, showing no fear, according to James G. Burrow, "that Government subsidization of training would lead to political domination of medicine."[7]

The AMA's response to the development of compulsory health insurance in Europe reflected its new progressive outlook. Prior to the passage of the National Insurance Act in Great Britain in 1911, the *Journal of the American Medical Association* (*JAMA*) displayed surprisingly little interest in the subject, a neglect especially remarkable in view of the literally thousands of American physicians who had personally observed the German system.[8]

The occasional references to German insurance are notable primarily for their ambivalence. While the benefits of health insurance were freely acknowledged, its effect on the medical profession was deplored. In an 1899 note on sickness insurance in Germany, one of the first to appear in *JAMA*, an editor concluded that "the whole scheme has proved practicable and far-reaching in its benefits, except to the medical profession, who are hampered and impoverished by the 'Kassen' rates and regulations and the abuses that creep in, and are constantly discussing measures to secure a uniform and equitable position in regard to them."[9] A decade later *JAMA* was still conveying the same message. Although social insurance has done "much to raise the level of comfort for working men and their families" in Germany, it observed, it has also had a negative effect on the practice and income of physicians.[10]

Foreign correspondents, writing from the major European capitals, kept *JAMA* readers current on developments abroad. For the most part, their reports were objective and constructive. The Vienna correspondent, for example, commenting in 1909 on a proposed Austrian Social Insurance Act, predicted that it would have a marked influence on "the general health and physical development of the masses." Despite the likelihood that the private practice of physicians would be curtailed, he thought the act had "undoubted advantages, both for the public and for the profession."[11]

The Berlin correspondent was equally open-minded. In reporting the efforts of German practitioners in 1910 to win free choice of physician

for patients—called "the American plan" by *JAMA*[12]—he sympathized with
the doctors' goals while simultaneously criticizing their tactics. When the
Krankenkassen committee of the German medical association accused the
government of "an unconcealed hostility to the medical profession," he
suggested that their indignation was "exaggerated."[13]

Early *JAMA* commentators frequently drew two conclusions from the
European experience: that health insurance was "bound to come" to America
and that American physicians could profit from the struggles of their
European "professional brethren," a favorite term of *JAMA* editor George
H. Simmons, a native Englishman.[14] In 1906 former AMA President Frank
Billings told a group of Chicago physicians that compulsory health insurance
was inevitable in the United States, regardless of what the medical profession
desired or of its economic consequences. While deploring the possible
"hardship" that it might impose on some physicians, he nevertheless predicted that compulsory health insurance would "have an influence in
preventing illness which every physician works for, and [that] the wholesome
effect of it on the community will be great."[15]

American physicians, confident that the United States would avoid the
worst of the European difficulties, were concerned about the financial loss
apparently suffered by many German doctors. But, as one *JAMA* editor
reassuringly noted, the problems plaguing the German profession were
neither "necessary or essential features of the compulsory insurance plan."
The Germans, not "being sufficiently alert to see the danger and sufficiently
well organized to resist it," had brought most of their troubles upon
themselves. "The lesson to us is obvious," the editor continued: American
physicians should be so well organized that the laws would prove to be a
blessing rather than a curse, and this could best be accomplished by joining
the revitalized AMA.[16] When compulsory health insurance came to America,
as it surely would, the editors of *JAMA* hoped that American doctors would
present a "united front and a moderate but positive" attitude in order "to
secure a living income before the inadequate compensation offered has
become crystallized into legislation."[17]

Following the introduction of Lloyd George's National Insurance Bill in
May 1911, American doctors began taking a keen interest in the topic of
compulsory health insurance. During the year and a half between the
introduction of the bill and the time its medical benefits went into effect,
London correspondents for both *JAMA* and the New York-based *Medical
Record* provided American readers with weekly progress reports on the
bill's passage through Parliament and blow-by-blow accounts of the British

Medical Association's fight for its famous "six points," including its threatened boycott of the system.[18] From these dispatches it seemed clear that the basic controversy between the government and the medical profession was over compensation and not—*JAMA* noted with some surprise —"over the principles on which the law is based."[19]

On this side of the Atlantic physicians tended to see the new law as much more than a novel business arrangement. The British law "is probably the most revolutionary, so far as medical practice is concerned, of any measure yet introduced in any English-speaking country," wrote a *JAMA* editor (probably Simmons) in 1912. It "marks the beginning of the end of the old system of the individual practice of medicine and of the old relationship between patient and physician—the beginning of a new era, both for society and for physicians." In the future, as the government assumed more and more responsibility for the health of its citizens, the physician would become "a health officer of the state, working for the general good, rather than as a private, professional or business man."[20] Surprisingly, the editor did not view this prospect with alarm. On the contrary, he saw it producing positive results: the elimination of charity work, the removal of mercenary motives for practicing medicine, the prevention of sickness among the poor, and a better quality of medical care. He also applauded the government's expanding role in providing health care. "The state in the future must protect the citizen against disease," he wrote, "just as it now protects him from foreign invasion."[21]

Speakers at the 65th anniversary meeting of the New York Academy of Medicine in 1912 expressed similar sentiments. In a session devoted to "The Doctor's Future," Algernon T. Bristow told the celebrants that compulsory health insurance would not only provide the poor with needed medical care, but would free physicians from the economic uncertainties of medical practice. The choice was clear: "We can either recognize the facts and meet them with advantage to ourselves as well as to the people we serve, or we may blindly shut our eyes to the facts and cry that it is unethical to attend people for a price that is within their means." These remarks prompted Abraham Jacobi, the venerable pediatrician and incumbent president of the AMA, to congratulate the Academy on "having fallen in line behind the economist and the reformer."[22]

American medical observers drew the same conclusions from developments in Great Britain that they had drawn earlier from Germany, only this time with greater conviction. The spread of compulsory health insurance to an English-speaking nation convinced many that its appearance in

America would not be far distant,[23] and the success of British physicians in winning many of their demands drove home the importance of a strong and united profession. "We may profitably and thoughtfully compare the magnificent activity of the British Medical Association and its constituent branches with the relative apathy and inaction shown by our own state and national organizations in this country when the material welfare of the medical profession is concerned," admonished the editor of the *New York State Journal of Medicine,* who noted with shame the large number of American physicians who were not members of the AMA.[24] Events in Great Britain had also demonstrated the value of good public relations. If British doctors had only cultivated the good will of the people, speculated one physician, they would have had no difficulty securing fair compensation.[25]

The medical benefits of the National Insurance Act began on January 15, 1913. To the surprise of many, on both sides of the Atlantic, the new plan worked remarkably well. Although there were frequent complaints about red tape and burdensome clerical work, reported *JAMA*'s London correspondent, the worst fears of the physicians had not materialized. Unnecessary night calls were few, and abuse of the system less than expected.[26] More important, many panel physicians were actually profiting under the act. "The situation is remarkable and unprecedented," exclaimed the correspondent.[27] Some doctors were working harder than ever before, but many practicing in poor industrial districts were doubling their incomes, and those in the more prosperous or rural areas were increasing theirs by 20 percent to 50 percent.[28] Panel practitioners expressed satisfaction with compulsory health insurance by nearly unanimously renewing their contracts at the expiration of the initial three months.[29]

Benefits to the nation were equally noticeable. "Millions" of poor people could now afford a physician for the first time, and qualified doctors were beginning to set up practices in working-class neighborhoods. But the act did retain "some of the evils inseparable from contract practice." Physicians occasionally gave perfunctory examinations and routine treatments, and hypochondriacs and malingerers sometimes took advantage of the system.[30] A government investigation of the latter, however, found "little, if any, evidence of fraud on the part of insured persons, or of deliberate malingering, but considerable evidence of a tendency to take the utmost advantage of the benefits under the act."[31] If the new law did not encourage thrift in prescribing drugs and supplies, it at least drastically reduced the sale of patent medicines.[32]

The positive results of the National Insurance Act encouraged a number of American physicians to call for similar legislation in this country or, as some phrased it, for the socialization of American medicine. Both economic and ethical considerations motivated them.[33] For the average practitioner, who, according to a Wisconsin physician, went into medicine primarily for "wealth and social position,"[34] the prospect of a fixed income and no outstanding bills might seem attractive.[35] But the most convincing argument for compulsory health insurance, in the opinion of *JAMA,* was "the failure of many persons in this country at present to receive medical care,"[36] which some physicians were coming to see as a basic right. "I believe," declared James P. Warbasse of New York,

that the wives of coal-miners and iron-workers are as worthy of the best scientific attention and the tenderest care in the hours of their need as are the wives of the rich. I believe that they should have it, not as a charity or welfare enterprise, but as a matter of social justice. It is their right.[37]

Although the AMA at this time had no official position on compulsory health insurance, the attitude of its most visible representatives was distinctly positive. George H. Simmons, an officer of the Association and editor of its *Journal* since 1899, was openly sympathetic to the health insurance system adopted by his native England.[38] Alexander Lambert, chairman of the Judicial Council, was similarly inclined. In his report at the annual session in 1915, he concluded that compulsory health insurance in Europe had been good for both doctor and patient and stopped just short of advocating it for this country.[39] Abraham Jacobi, president in 1912 and 1913, also favored it. But the person most responsible for the AMA's early commitment to compulsory health insurance was Frederick R. Green, an 1898 graduate of the North-western University Medical School, who had joined the AMA in 1905 as assistant secretary and then moved up in 1910 to become secretary and executive officer of the newly created Council on Health and Public Instruction.[40]

Green's friendship with the advocates of compulsory health insurance went back at least to 1912, when the AALL and the AMA had collaborated on a National Conference on Industrial Disease. The following April Green and John B. Andrews had jointly sponsored a meeting at AALL headquarters, where plans were discussed to coordinate activities relating to public health legislation. Not much came of the meeting, but Green and Andrews continued to stay in touch with each other.[41] On occasion, the AALL secretary

Fig. 8. Frederick R. Green (Irving Fisher and Eugene L. Fisk, *How to Live*, New York: Funk & Wagnalls, 1915).

even used Green as a conduit to the medical profession. In August 1914, for example, he sent Green an announcement of the AALL's plans for health insurance legislation and suggested that he prepare a *JAMA* editorial on the subject.[42]

Thus Andrews was not approaching a stranger when in November 1915 he sent Green a copy of the tentative draft, together with an editorial he had written for *JAMA* and a press release he had prepared for the AMA.[43] Nevertheless, Green's enthusiastic response must have come as a welcome surprise. The AALL's plan for compulsory health insurance, wrote the AMA official,

is exactly in line with the views that I have held for a long time regarding the methods which should be followed in securing public health legislation. . . . Your plans are so entirely in line with our own that I want to be of every possible assistance. I have followed the development of industrial insurance in England since the introduction and passage of Lloyd George's National Insurance Act and have from time to time through JOURNAL editorials and otherwise warned the medical profession in this country that the time was soon coming when it would be necessary to consider very seriously the relation of physicians to industrial insurance in this country.

Green then went on to congratulate the AALL's Committee on Social Insurance for their handling of the medical provisions of the bill and for seeking the advice of Alexander Lambert, "who probably knows more about this subject than any other physician in the country."[44]

Although Lambert was chairman of the AMA's Judicial Council and thus could easily serve as an unofficial liason between the AMA and the AALL, Green was not satisfied. He wanted to give the AALL "the assistance and backing of the American Medical Association in some official way and to devise some plan by which the Association can be officially represented in the development of your model law." He proposed to have the Council on Health and Public Instruction, of which he was secretary, appoint a special committee to work with the AALL on "such questions as compensation, choice of physicians on the part of the insured, manner of preparation of lists of physicians to furnish medical services under the law, manner in which patients shall be assigned to these physicians, surgical operations, hospital care, etc."[45]

Specifically, he wanted the committee to consist of Lambert; Henry B. Favill, a socially minded Chicago physician who was chairman of the Council on Health and Public Instruction; and a third physician, "preferably one located in New York or near by, who with Lambert would constitute a majority of such committee" and who could work closely with the AALL on the medical details of the model bill. "This," wrote Green, "would guarantee the proper representation of physicians in the formulation of these plans." If Andrews liked his idea, Green promised to suggest it to Lambert, Favill, and A. R. Craig, the AMA's secretary. He closed his letter with a request for twenty-five additional copies of the tentative draft, one for each member of the Judicial Council and the Council on Health and Public Instruction.[46]

Green was as good as his word. The November 20 issue of *JAMA* carried an editorial—perhaps a version of the one Andrews had submitted —describing the AALL's bill and praising the AALL for consulting physicians before including any medical provisions.[47] In the meantime Green, apparently with Andrews' approval, arranged with Craig, Favill, and Lambert to set up an advisory committee, with Lambert as chairman and Favill as a member. At Lambert's suggestion, Frederic J. Cotton, a Boston surgeon who for several years had chaired the Committee on Compensation of the Massachusetts State Medical Society, was appointed the third member.[48]

The announcement in *JAMA* of the committee's formation, undoubtedly prepared by Green, noted that the subject of compulsory health insurance had left "the realm of academic discussion" and was now "in the front rank of the pressing practical questions confronting the medical profession." In fact, the writer predicted that compulsory health insurance would be "the next step in health legislation." Because of the "certainty that such laws will be enacted within a few years, the success of the American Association for Labor Legislation in obtaining the legislation it advocates, and the consideration shown to the medical profession," it was explained, the Council on Health and Public Instruction had decided that cooperation with the AALL was both "desirable and opportune."[49]

On February 9, 1916, the AMA board of trustees approved the establishment of a Committee on Social Insurance and instructed its members to undertake

the careful compilation of information in *re* social or health insurance and the relations of physicians thereto; and to do everything in their power to secure such constructions of the proposed laws as will work the most harmonious adjustment of the new sociologic relations between physicians and laymen which will necessarily result therefrom.[50]

The trustees also authorized a first-year budget of $6,000 for the committee and granted it permission "to carry on its work wherever seems most desirable."[51] The most desirable location turned out to be in New York City, in the same building that housed the AALL. On May 1, 1916, the AMA hired I. M. Rubinow as executive secretary of its Social Insurance Committee and installed him in an office close to his AALL associates.[52] With the chairman and executive secretary of the AMA's Committee on Social Insurance serving simultaneously on the AALL's committee, physicians and Progressives formed a united front for the forthcoming campaign for compulsory health insurance.

4. THE OPENING ROUND

Whether one likes it or not, social health insurance is bound to come sooner or later, and it behooves the medical profession to meet this condition with dignity. . . . Blind condemnation will lead nowhere and may bring about a repetition of the humiliating experiences suffered by the medical profession in some of the European countries.

Editorial in the Medical Record, *March 1916*

In January 1916, after three years of investigation and education, the AALL began the legislative phase of its campaign for compulsory health insurance. The time was not auspicious. The nation's enthusiasm for reform was waning, and the war in Europe was diverting the attention of many from domestic to foreign issues. Nevertheless, AALL leaders anticipated quick passage of their model bill. Their optimism was so great, in fact, they decided to forego requesting the establishment of state investigating commissions and to introduce their bill immediately in three populous industrial states of the East: New York, Massachusetts, and New Jersey. The AALL pinned its greatest hopes on New York, home of the largest—and generally best informed—state medical association in the country.

The New York campaign began on January 24, when State Senator Ogden L. Mills introduced a revised version of the AALL's model bill in the Senate. The Mills bill, as it was called, differed in two important respects from the first tentative draft. First, in the interest of economy and simplified actuarial procedures, medical care for the families of insured persons had been deleted, although families were still eligible for voluntary enrollment. Second, because of the "violent opposition" of Florence Kelley, general secretary of the National Consumers' League, the eight-week cash maternity benefit for women workers had been dropped. Kelley, it seems, feared that the lure of cash payments would induce husbands to force their pregnant wives into employment. Either all women should be eligible for the cash benefit, she argued, or none at all. Although the AALL rejected her reasoning —"it is economic necessity and not idle husbands which drives women to seek employment outside of their homes," replied Olga Halsey—it capitulated to her demand that the provision be omitted.[1]

Early physician reaction to the proposed bill centered on the absence of specific medical provisions, especially for the payment of doctors, which

37

the AALL planned to add after further consultation with the medical profession. This bill, complained Eden V. Delphey of New York City, "seems to have been drafted either as though [physicians] did not exist, or that they were of absolutely of no importance in the scheme of things."[2] Delphey, a former pharmacist who had practiced medicine for a quarter century among the wage-earners of New York, was vice president of the Federation of Medical Economics Leagues, a trade union of New York physicians, and the self-appointed spokesman for the general practitioners of the state.[3] Although he found the Mills bill unacceptable, he was not opposed to compulsory health insurance legislation that contained "five fundamental propositions": adequate medical representation on all decision-making bodies, open panels, free choice of physician, contracts made directly with participating doctors, and impartial referees paid by the state to rule on cash benefits.[4]

The attitude of the New York medical press was generally similar to Delphey's: negative toward certain features of the Mills bill, but positive toward the principle of compulsory health insurance. The *Long Island Medical Journal,* edited by H. G. Webster, was perhaps the most supportive. "Any step to provide adequate medical attendance is a long step in advance," wrote the editor, whose chief concern was the remuneration of physicians. "If the proposed bill is to bring to workmen a good class of medical attendance and nursing," he explained, "the first requisite is an adequate return that will attract thoroughly qualified practitioners of medicine."[5]

The *Medical Record* of New York City acknowledged that the Mills bill contained some "undesirable features," but thought these could easily be corrected. In the meantime, it urged physicians to refrain from hasty denunciations:

Whether one likes it or not, social health insurance is bound to come sooner or later, and it behooves the medical profession to meet this condition with dignity and to insist firmly and without heat that a measure designed to benefit and strengthen the social fabric of the community should deal fairly with the physician on whom its eventual success must of necessity depend. Blind condemnation will lead nowhere and may bring about a repetition of the humiliating experiences suffered by the medical profession in some of the European countries.[6]

The *Buffalo Medical Times* feared that some of the bill's provisions might prove deleterious to the practice of medicine, but supported its "general principle."[7] The *Albany Medical Annals* simply reported the introduction of the bill with no editorial comment.[8]

The most hostile response came from the *New York Medical Journal*, which professed admiration for the intention of the Mills bill while deploring its likely consequences. The proposed legislation, it believed, threatened "to lower the self respect of every worker, debase medical standards, promote litigation, foster the vices of simulation and perjury, and impose enormous and useless expense upon the State." Instead of improving the public health, it would endanger it by placing "a premium on low grade medical service and medical place hunting."[9] Such editorial comments lent credence to the opinion of William S. Gottheil that, although most New York physicians knew little more than the name of the health insurance bill, medical opposition was "crystallising rapidly."[10]

The first medical organization to take official action on the Mills bill was the Medical Society of the County of New York. At its February meeting Samuel J. Kopetzky, chairman of the Committee on Legislation, read a report sharply critical of the proposed legislation. Since the committee was confident that insurance was coming regardless of its wishes, it chose not to raise the question of desirability but instead to offer specific criticisms and suggestions. In the committee's opinion, the bill protected the interests of neither patient nor physician. It ignored the crucial issue of how physicians would be paid, made no provision for screening out unqualified practitioners, and incorporated "the worse evils of contract practice," that is, it encouraged physicians "to treat large numbers of patients at minimum rates." An acceptable bill would include:

1. The minimum wage of the physician taking up this kind of contract practice.
2. The maximum number of persons to be placed under a given contract practitioner's care.
3. The appointment of medical physicians under these contracts should be made only after Civil Service examination to qualify the practitioner and should be limited to those qualified to practice under the Medical Practice Laws of this State.[11]

Despite S. S. Goldwater's appeal to delay action, the society voted to accept Kopetzky's report.[12]

This action impressed many individuals—both physicians and laymen—as premature and self-serving. The *New York Times* denounced the New York County physicians for being "mere obstructionists," concerned only with their own financial well-being.[13] The *Medical Record* called the action "ill-timed and ill-advised."[14] And the editors of *American Medicine* offered a stern rebuke. It seemed to them that the society's opposition stemmed primarily from the absence of a fee schedule, and they thought it was "exceedingly unfortunate that in these days of social progress, a representative medical society should reject with an air of finality a measure designed to better health conditions in the state." Physicians, they urged, should "rally to its support, encourage its progress, and facilitate its wide extension throughout the states where laws of this character have not been enacted." In so doing, they would contribute not only to the public welfare, but to their own pocketbooks as well.[15]

In March the New York Senate Judiciary Committee held public hearings on the Mills bill, attended by a number of physicians and AALL officers including Andrews, Rubinow, and Lambert, who also represented the AMA's Social Insurance Committee. Most of the physicians present testified against the bill, but many of them—to the surprise of the AALL representatives—also spoke favorably of compulsory health insurance. Although the medical profession appeared "technically on the side of the opposition," observed Olga Halsey, their effort "to protect their interests and those of the future insured workmen reveals the rapid progress that health insurance has made in the thinking of the medical profession." Their constructive proposals, she thought, were stimulated in large measure by the conviction that some health insurance bill would soon become law.[16]

The physicians opposing the Mills bill, led by Delphey, were equally pleased with their performance in Albany. On the train back to New York City Delphey and Chamberlain, who had drafted the legislation, shared a seat and discussed their respective positions. The doctor seemed especially anxious to avoid having to negotiate with a plethora of local mutual funds and preferred a more easily controlled state insurance fund. He also displayed considerable antipathy toward Goldwater, one of the most outspoken and frequently quoted physicians supporting the bill. According to Chamberlain, Delphey resented "Goldwater's encroachments on the territory of the practicing physicians," arguing that since the former health commissioner was "a mere hospital administrator" he could not speak for the medical profession.[17]

In an apparent move to buy time, James F. Rooney, an Albany physician representing the state medical society, recommended that the legislature appoint a commission to investigate "the whole question of Health Insurance."[18] The AALL, convinced by the hearings that their bill stood little chance of passage in 1916, acquiesced.[19] Senator Mills feared that the war in Europe would impede a thorough investigation, but AALL leaders assured him that sufficient data relating to the European experience were already on

Fig. 9. James F. Rooney (Courtesy of the
Medical Society of the State of New
York).

hand.[20] Consequently on March 29 Mills introduced a substitute bill, prepared
by the AALL, calling for the establishment of "a commission to investigate
sickness and accidents among employees in the State of New York and
make an appropriation therefor." Three weeks later this measure passed the
Senate by a large margin and was sent on to the Assembly, where it
apparently died in committee.[21]

Despite the legislature's failure even to appoint an investigative commission, no one believed that the debate over compulsory health insurance
had ended. The AALL immediately began laying plans for 1917, while
critics of the Mills bill, resigned to the passage of some insurance legislation,
planned their strategy. The hostile *New York Medical Journal,* which greeted
the bill's temporary demise with the comment "de mortuis nil nisi bonum,"
advised physicians not to oppose future bills "but to see that they are fair to
all concerned."[22] Similarly, the *Long Island Medical Journal* urged the
medical profession to "begin actively at once to protect its just rights and to
see that the proper safeguards shall be incorporated in the next draft of the
bill."[23]

By the time this advice appeared, the Medical Society of the State of
New York was doing just that. On March 15 its Council, at Lambert's
suggestion, appointed a special health insurance committee composed of

James F. Rooney, chairman of the society's Committee on Legislation, as chairman; Samuel J. Kopetzky, chairman of the Committee on Legislation of the New York County Medical Society; James N. Vander Veer; Franklin C. Gram; and Frank Van Fleet, a New York City physician who regarded the Mills bill as "one of the most iniquitous and unjust efforts that have as yet been made to place class legislation on the statute books."[24]

Throughout the spring and summer of 1916 members of the committee met collectively and individually with representatives of the AALL to work out medical provisions acceptable to the medical profession. The physicians did not insist on a guaranteed minimum wage, but they did want a limit on size of panels, free choice of physician, adequate medical representation on administrative bodies, and supervision of medical services.[25] The AALL was generally willing to meet the physicians more than halfway, but it did not want to concede too much too fast. "I think it is just as well when dealing with these doctors," counseled Chamberlain, "not to feed them out the whole of the material at once but rather give them a part and then a little more later."[26]

By autumn the AALL and the state medical society (now represented by Kopetzky's Committee on Medical Economics, which apparently assumed the duties of the temporary Health Insurance Committee chaired by Rooney) had reached agreement on several key issues. In order to avoid the worst "evils" of the much-despised contract practice, medical service under the proposed act was to be provided by panels

of physicians to which all legally qualified physicians shall have the right to belong, and from among whom the patients shall have free choice of physician, subject to the physician's right to refuse patients on grounds specified in regulations made under this act; provided, however, that no physician on the panel shall have on his list of insured patients more than 500 insured families nor more than 1,000 insured individuals.[27]

Salaried medical officers, appointed to oversee the act, were "to examine patients who claim cash benefit, to provide a certificate of disability, and to supervise the character of the medical service in the interests of insured patients, physicians, and carriers." Finally, the physicians were promised representation on the State Social Insurance Commission and on other administrative bodies.[28]

Several payment plans were discussed, but either the physicians or the reformers objected to each one. The capitation plan of paying physicians a fixed sum per person per year, used in Great Britain and in contract practices, had the drawback of sometimes encouraging "neglectful hurried service to the patients." Paying salaries to participating physicians would necessitate restricting the size of panels and, consequently, the patient's freedom of choice. Most practitioners preferred a fee-for-service plan based on approved schedules, which would pay them for the actual amount of work done and thus, in theory at least, encourage them to give each patient careful attention. But this plan was difficult to control and potentially expensive. To control expenditures, the AALL suggested a compromise between capitation and fee-for-service, in which "a total sum, calculated on the per capita basis, is distributed among physicians in accordance with the services rendered by each." This arrangement, however, would tend to compensate physicians less the more work they did.[29]

On November 23, at a special meeting in New York City called by the Committee on Medical Economics, Kopetzky announced that the state medical society's previous objections to the Mills bill "have now been met," with both public and professional interests well protected. This endorsement was particularly significant, since Kopetzky had earlier, in February, authored the report of the New York County Medical Society condemning the Mills bill.[30]

Not all physicians, however, were appeased. To Eden Delphey, the basic question was not what working conditions the medical profession was willing to accept, but whether or not any compulsory health insurance system was desirable. Were doctors, he asked, ready to give up their individuality and professional identity and become mere cogs "in the great medical machine?" Were they willing to gamble away their independence for the uncertain possibility of economic gain? If health insurance were so desirable, then why limit it to manual laborers? Why not "insure every man, woman and child, whether they pay any part of the cost or not on the same ground and for the same purpose that the State furnishes free schooling, free water, and free fire and police protection?" Apparently unaware of recent AALL concessions, Delphey insisted, as a bare minimum, on five "fundamental propositions": adequate representation, open panels, free choice of physician, impartial referees, and—above all—collective bargaining.[31] All but the last demand had already been granted.

Such objections notwithstanding, Kopetzky at the next meeting of the Council of the state medical society introduced a resolution acknowledging the changes made by the AALL in its model bill and officially endorsing the revised draft:

. . . Be It Resolved, That the Council of the Medical Society of the State of New York, considering that these essentials safeguard the public interest, the public health, and the welfare of the medical profession, hereby endorses and approves the Medical Provisions of the tentative draft of the Compulsory Health Insurance Act, and instructs its Committee on Medical Economics in conjunction with its Committee on Legislation to act in accordance with these resolutions.

After "extended discussion"—and over the written protest of Rooney, who was absent—the Council approved this resolution.[32] The AALL thus concluded the first round of its New York campaign on an optimistic note. It had failed to win passage of the original model bill, but it had apparently won the support of the most powerful and influential medical organization in the state.

In Massachusetts the story was much the same, but with less drama. On January 14, 1916, Representative Albert M. Chandler introduced the model bill, which in Massachusetts came to be known as the Doten bill, after its sponsor, Carroll W. Doten, a statistician at the Massachusetts Institute of Technology and a member of the AALL's Committee on Social Insurance. Unlike the vocal New York physicians, the medical profession in Massachusetts greeted the bill with virtual silence, which the AALL interpreted as a sign of failure to recognize the true importance of the measure.[33]

On March 1 the Massachusetts legislature held hearings on compulsory health insurance in chambers overflowing with interested spectators. Among those testifying in favor of the bill were Doten; Michael M. Davis, Jr., superintendent of the Boston Dispensary; Mary Beard of the District Nurses' Association; and two prominent Boston physicians: Frederic J. Cotton, a member of the AMA's Social Insurance Committee, and Richard C. Cabot, of the Massachusetts General Hospital. In Cotton's opinion, the consensus was that compulsory health insurance was "inevitable."[34] He was less sure, however, that it was desirable, especially for physicians. But as long as it seemed likely to provide medical care of high quality to those otherwise unable to receive it, he would not be inclined to oppose the measure.[35]

In view of the developing interest in compulsory health insurance and the need to safeguard the interests of the profession, the Council of the Massachusetts Medical Society in June appointed a Committee on Industrial Health Insurance, consisting of Cotton and two other members. The Council specifically instructed the committee to "use their best efforts to prevent the taking away from the practitioners of the State the privilege of attending their own private cases," a prospect the AALL had not even considered.[36] On October 4 the committee brought back a report generally favorable to the principle of compulsory health insurance, provided that physicians would be paid per visit and not on a capitation basis.[37]

Meanwhile, the legislature had decided to sidestep voting on the Doten bill and instead to appoint a recess committee to study the issue.[38] When this committee announced plans to hold hearings in early October, the AALL began making careful plans to insure a favorable outcome. Staff members spent days talking with editors around the state and lining up speakers to endorse the bill. They were chagrined, however, when despite their efforts five members of the Massachusetts Medical Society, including their erstwhile ally Cotton, proceeded to "doublecross" them. "It is perfectly apparent," complained a bitter John Andrews, "that the doctors in Massachusetts know little about Health Insurance and less about what they really want themselves."[39]

Andrews' outburst was fair neither to Cotton, who remained basically loyal to the cause of health insurance, nor to the Massachusetts medical profession as a whole. The state's most influential medical journal, the *Boston Medical and Surgical Journal,* openly supported the AALL's cause even though it stopped short of actually endorsing the Doten bill.[40] The physicians of Massachusetts, it predicted, would "be benefited rather than injured by a proper sickness insurance act," and it urged "a kindly and sympathetic as well as critical attitude on the part of the medical profession."[41] In fact the *Journal* was so favorably inclined toward the proposed bill, one irate practitioner accused it of becoming a self-appointed "champion" of the measure, in opposition to the wishes of "the great majority of the profession" in his part of the state.[42]

In December Cotton, as chairman, reported the findings of the Committee on Industrial Health Insurance. Instead of taking a position on the value of compulsory health insurance itself, he and his colleagues had drawn up a list of "provisions that represent what we may call the irreducible minimum of medical rights." These included limiting the number of insured patients a physician could serve to 500 families or 2,000 individuals—double the number of persons the AALL's revised bill allowed—and paying participating doctors on a fee-per-visit basis according to a schedule "not less than the average minimum fee for services rendered by physicians and surgeons of the locality in similar cases."[43] Later that month the Council of the state medical society passed a carefully worded resolution neither approving nor condemning compulsory health insurance, but recommending only that passage be delayed:

Resolved, That realizing the importance of the proposed Health Insurance Laws for Massachusetts, and appreciating the great change that would come in the social conditions of the people of the State, and appreciating further the great role the medical profession would play in the proper administration of such laws, and feeling that the citizens of Massachusetts should be more fully informed as to the scope and meaning of the proposed legislation, we, the Council of the Massachusetts Medical Society, assembled in meeting for the purpose of considering health insurance, most respectfully request that no definite plan on Health Insurance or recommendation in regard to health insurance, be submitted to the Legislature, until a further knowledge of the proposed Laws be spread among the citizens of the Commonwealth.[44]

The AALL's failure to win an endorsement from the Massachusetts Medical Society was more than offset by its successes with the medical societies of Pennsylvania and Wisconsin, the third and thirteenth largest state medical associations in the nation. Wisconsin physicians took an early interest in the health insurance debate. At its annual meeting in 1914, a full year before the AALL even published its tentative draft, the State Medical Society of Wisconsin scheduled two papers calling for increased government involvement in providing health care.[45] The following year President T. J. Redelings predicted the coming of compulsory health insurance within the decade and urged Wisconsin physicians to lead the movement.[46] As a first step in this direction the incoming president, Louis Jermain, appointed a seven-man interim Committee on Health Insurance, chaired by H. E. Dearholt, a Milwaukee physician who served as executive secretary of the Wisconsin Anti-Tuberculosis Association.[47]

Delegates to the 1916 annual session of the State Medical Society of Wisconsin fairly brimmed with enthusiasm for compulsory health insurance. The AALL's model bill had already been introduced in three states, and Jermain took the opportunity in his presidential address to advocate co-operating with the state legislature in formulating such legislation for Wisconsin.[48] The interim committee, in what it modestly called "a mere introduction to the subject," reported favorably on compulsory health insurance. Unlike most other American physicians, who preferred being paid on a fee-for-service basis, these Wisconsin practitioners recommended payment on a per capita basis, with free choice of any physician on the panel.[49] The day after he presented this report, the chairman, Dearholt, was elected president of the society, an honor he saw as more of "a triumph for social medicine" than a personal recognition.[50]

Later that same day the widespread support for compulsory health insurance was tangibly demonstrated with a formal endorsement by the House of Delegates. As the meeting was about to adjourn, W. F. Zierath, a member of the Health Insurance Committee from Sheboygan, introduced the following resolution:

> *Be it resolved,* By the House of Delegates of the State Medical Society of Wisconsin, that we commend the principle of compulsory health insurance, and that we pledge our support in the enactment of that principle into law.

The resolution passed without a single dissenting vote.[51]

Just a month earlier the House of Delegates of the Medical Society of the State of Pennsylvania had passed a similar resolution, introduced by F. L. Van Sickle:

> *Resolved,* That the work of the American Association for Labor Legislation be endorsed and that the tentative draft of a health insurance bill be favored as a model bill were such to come before the legislature of Pennsylvania.[52]

Important as these endorsements were, they may not have reflected accurately the feelings of the majority of Wisconsin and Pennsylvania practitioners. In Pennsylvania it was noted that few doctors, even in Philadelphia and Pittsburgh, knew much about compulsory health insurance and that its support was coming primarily from a handful of "outstanding leaders."[53] The same may well have been true in Wisconsin.

Two other states showing considerable interest in compulsory health insurance were Illinois and California, where Governor Hiram Johnson had appointed a Social Insurance Commission in September 1915, months before the AALL's bill was introduced in the East.[54] The *California State Journal of Medicine,* which had anticipated such action, responded positively, especially in editorials by René Bine of San Francisco, who declared that universal health insurance was not only "inevitable but desirable."[55] In April, at the suggestion of the state investigating commission, the Medical Society of the State of California appointed a Committee on Social Insurance, with the pro-insurance Bine as chairman.[56] Bine's committee held numerous meetings and generally tried to arouse the state's physicians to become familiar with the basic issues of health insurance.[57]

On July 1 the state commission secured the services of I. M. Rubinow, who took a six-month leave of absence from the AMA to serve as an expert in California.[58] His presence in the state, where he was a frequent speaker at meetings of both physicians and laymen, gave increased visibility to health insurance.[59] At a meeting of the San Francisco County Medical Society in September he participated in a discussion of the issue with two local physicians, James L. Whitney, a general practitioner who favored health insurance, and John H. Graves, president of the county society, who opposed it. Whitney thought the medical profession would support insurance legislation because it seemed to be "the only practical and just means of ending an intolerable economic situation," and because it could be "the means of furthering the necessary development of medical practice along the lines of co-operation."[60] His comments elicited only praise from Rubinow. Graves' opposition stemmed from economic concerns. He had heard that German doctors had been forced to strike to get paid even 25 cents to 35 cents per visit, and he feared that if a similar system were instituted in California it would drive out all the "active and alert" minds, leaving "only the dolts and dreamers to worship at the shrine of Hippocrates."[61] Rubinow, who disapproved of anyone entering the medical profession for financial gain, pointed out that physicians would probably benefit financially under health insurance, since it would eliminate charity work and uncollectable bills.[62]

Not all those present found Rubinow's arguments—or Whitney's—convincing. Donald M. Gedge could scarcely remember being offered "such a feast of theoretical and fantastical viands." Isn't it strange, he asked, "that nearly all of the so-called social uplifters, especially of the male persuasion, should be of foreign birth, who find their chief occupation centered in administering to the delinquencies of our foreign population?" In years of practice the only poverty he had seen "was almost invariably due to improvidence, intemperance, immorality, and utter disregard for ordinary industry," and the worthy poor had always received "the very best medical aid." Compulsory health insurance, he concluded, was

an assault upon the rights of every man practicing medicine in the State of California, and should be met with united and determined opposition by every medical man of every school of practice throughout the land. It is an attempt to enslave the profession, to deprive it of its just rights and privileges; and, under the cloak of charity, is selfishly catering to the aggrandizement of a few Socialists and dreamers. Let them prophesy for us as gloomily as they wish, and let them proclaim in the *ipse dixit* platitudes of idealists as they may; the world is a practical problem and we still have it within us to oppose and finally defeat them, but it can only be accomplished by concentrated and united action. *Fideli Certa Merces.*[63]

Fig. 10. Edward H. Ochsner (*Bulletin of the Linn County Medical Society*, 1937, 6: 5).

By the time the Social Insurance Commission held public hearings in November, the state medical society still had not taken a stand on health insurance; so the physicians who testified did so strictly as individuals.[64] Rubinow, as the commission's expert, examined many of the witnesses, including Dr. Graves, with whom he had clashed in San Francisco. This time Rubinow took the opportunity to wring from his reluctant witness a concession that the quality of medical care and the caliber of physicians in Germany had not generally suffered as a result of health insurance. In another exchange Rubinow argued that most physicians, though perhaps "suspicious" about the consequences of compulsory health insurance, felt that it was "in a general way a good measure, a measure that is rather essential to the welfare of a certain class of people who, in the community, are unable to get proper medical service, because of the extraordinary burden that is imposed upon them by any prolonged illness."[65] His knowledgeable performance at these hearings no doubt left many California voters with a positive impression of compulsory health insurance.

Illinois physicians, who would later play a crucial role in the health insurance debate, paid little attention to the subject until late in 1916, when it appeared likely that a bill would soon be introduced in the Illinois legislature. Except for the *Illinois Medical Journal,* which branded compulsory health insurance as paternalistic and un-American, the initial response in Illinois was positive.[66] On December 21 the West Side Branch of the Chicago Medical Society sponsored a meeting devoted to "Social Insurance Legislation." Of the nine persons who participated either as speakers or discussants, "five were definitely in favor of compulsory health insurance, three expressed the opinion that it was bound to come and the best thing to do for the medical profession was to get the best terms they could," and only one, a local surgeon named Edward H. Ochsner, opposed the idea.[67] Ochsner, an 1894 graduate of Rush Medical College, had studied in Austria and Germany during the late 1890s, and a six-week stint as an assistant to a panel physician in Leipzig had left him with an indelible distaste for compulsory health insurance. In 1897 he returned to Chicago, where for years he served as attending surgeon at Augustana Hospital.[68] Within a short time of his maiden speech in Chicago, he would emerge as the Midwest's most effective and vocal opponent of compulsory health insurance.

Judged by most criteria, the AALL's 1916 state-by-state campaign was a success. No state had passed the model bill, but several had set up commissions to study the need for it. No state medical society had taken a stand against insurance, while two had officially endorsed it, and at least six more had established health insurance committees.[69] Virtually all informed physicians seemed convinced that compulsory health insurance was inevitable, and many hoped that it would substantially increase their incomes.

The great mass of the medical profession, however, remained apathetic to the issue. Late in the year Eden Delphey polled the secretaries of every state medical society. The thirty-two replies yielded the following information:

1. Has the matter of Compulsory, or any other kind of Health Insurance, ever been formally brought before your State Society? Yes, 9; no, 23.
2. Has your State Society ever taken any action, either pro or con, regarding it? Favorable, 2; committees, 6; no, 24.
3. Did your State Society instruct its delegates to the American Medical Association Annual Meeting held at Detroit, June 12-16, 1916—either pro or con regarding Health Insurance? No, 32.
4. Do you know what is the sentiment of the medical profession in your state regarding Health Insurance? Favorable, 2; unfavorable, 4; doubtful, 1; sub-judice, 1; don't know, 24.
5. Do you consider the second "Tentative draft" issued by the A.A.L.L. to be just

and fair to the medical profession? Yes, 3; no, 5; doubtful, 1; don't know, 23.

6. What do you consider to be the best form of Health Insurance—providing some form of Health Insurance is inevitable? By employer, employee, and State, 2; like compensation insurance, 1; free choice, good compensation, 1; don't know, 28.

7. Do you think that inasmuch as the State must pay the expense eventually, anyway, that it would be better to have the State take over the matter of Health Insurance and insure every man, woman, and child earning under a specified sum per annum, whether they paid any assessments or not, on the same principle that the State furnishes common school education? Would this plan be better, simpler, and cheaper than the various plans so far promulgated? Yes, 4; no, 3; probably, 2; don't know, 23.[70]

Clearly, American physicians had not yet made up their minds about compulsory health insurance.

5. THE NEXT GREAT STEP

... there are unmistakable signs that health insurance will constitute the next great step in social legislation.

Dr. Rupert Blue, President of the AMA, June, 1916

No other social movement in modern economic development is so pregnant with benefit to the public.

Editorial, JAMA, *May, 1916*

National discussions of compulsory health insurance in 1916 were just as positive as those on the state level. Following the appointment of the AMA's Committee on Social Insurance, *JAMA* continued to lend its support to the movement, greeting the introduction of legislation in New York and Massachusetts with the observation that "much of the best informed opinion of the country is in favor of these proposals."[1] Ostensibly the *Journal* only wanted to arouse the profession to the need for a united front in order to avoid the unseemly conflicts that had occurred abroad, but its editorials were hardly neutral. "No other social movement in modern economic development is so pregnant with benefit to the public," declared one.[2] The appearance of the AALL bill, said another, marks "the inauguration of a great movement which ought to result in an improvement in the health of the industrial population and improve the conditions for medical service among the wage earners."[3]

The AMA's friendliness toward health insurance was particularly evident at the Association's annual session in June 1916. President Rupert Blue, surgeon general of the United States Public Health Service, set the tone in his presidential address by referring to compulsory health insurance as "the next great step in social legislation"—a slogan the AALL quickly splashed across the bottom of its stationery.[4] Alexander Lambert, chairman of the Committee on Social Insurance, presented the delegates with a "voluminous report" on the activities of his committee and on the operation of European insurance plans. Although the committee, like *JAMA,* professed neutrality, its enthusiasm for compulsory health insurance was scarcely concealed. Its lengthy account of the European experience, prepared largely by Rubinow, concluded with the statement that "however one may criticize

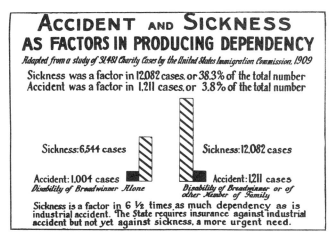

ACCIDENT AND SICKNESS AS FACTORS IN PRODUCING DEPENDENCY

Adapted from a study of 31,481 Charity Cases by the United States Immigration Commission, 1909

Sickness was a factor in 12,082 cases. or 38.3% of the total number
Accident was a factor in 1,211 cases. or 3.8% of the total number

Sickness: 6,544 cases

Sickness: 12,082 cases

Accident: 1,004 cases
Disability of Breadwinner Alone

Accident: 1,211 cases
Disability of Breadwinner or of other Member of Family

Sickness is a factor in 6 ½ times as much dependency as is industrial accident. The State requires insurance against industrial accident but not yet against sickness, a more urgent need.

Fig. 11. From *American Labor Legislation Review,* 1916, *6:* facing p. 179.

the details, the insurance act [in Europe] has unquestionably improved the condition of the working classes which have come under the law."[5]

The committee's full-time executive secretary, Rubinow, devoted virtually all his considerable energies to the cause of health insurance. Although on loan to the California Social Insurance Commission for the last half of 1916, he continued to represent the AMA and to push it in the direction of endorsing compulsory health insurance.[6] Without doubt he was the most visible partisan of the measure in America. In addition to preparing most of the annual report of the Committee on Social Insurance, he published a major book on the subject, prepared a series of pamphlets for the AMA, "traveled nearly 22,000 miles, addressed over 100 meetings with a combined audience of nearly 50,000, personally met thousands of people interested in the movement and, of course, talked and was spoken to with reference to little else besides this one subject."[7]

In his public appearances Rubinow effectively contrasted the plight of America's poor with their counterparts in Europe. Speaking to a California audience, he related the case of the "C" family in New York City. An attack of pneumonia forced Mr. C. to quit his job for several months. There were four children to feed, and his wife's job was gradually destroying her vision. One hundred and fifty dollars would save her sight, but the C's had no savings and no insurance. "Suppose for a moment," said Rubinow, "that the C. family was living in monarchial Leipzig rather than in democratic

America." There the sickness fund would have provided Mr. C. with the necessary medical and hospital care, and given the C. family financial support for up to thirty-two weeks, thus allowing Mrs. C. to stay home with her family and preserve her vision. Such, he said, "is the case of health insurance in a nutshell."[8]

Throughout the year Rubinow's colleagues at the AALL, particularly John Andrews, were also campaigning energetically for compulsory health insurance. Between January and May Andrews and his staff gave thirty speeches, sent 53,400 letters, mailed 64,800 pieces of literature, prepared fifty press releases, made 2,692 phone calls, and wrote a miscellany of articles.[9] In June, Andrews visited Illinois, Wisconsin, and Michigan, where in Detroit he lobbied with notable success among the physicians gathered for the jointly held annual sessions of the AMA, the American Academy of Medicine, which specialized in "medical sociology," and the newly organized American Association of Physicians and Surgeons, composed of about 250 practitioners primarily associated with industrial medicine. From each of these bodies he won a promise to assist "in putting the finishing touches on the [model] bill."[10] Following the passage on August 19 of the Kern-McGillicuddy bill, compensating injured federal employees, he devoted "even greater attention" to the promotion of health insurance.[11]

At its annual meeting in December the AALL featured several sessions on compulsory health insurance. Of the papers presented, perhaps the most important was Alexander Lambert's on "Medical Organization under Health Insurance." According to his scheme, open panels would provide medical treatment to the insured, who would be free to choose any panel practitioner willing to accept him. Practices would be limited to about 500 families or 1,000 individuals. The physicians, as well as the health department and the attending staffs of dispensaries and hospitals, would elect representatives to local medical committees, which would conduct all negotiations with the insurance fund directors.[12]

To avoid placing panel physicians in the uncomfortable position of deciding who was eligible for cash benefits, the funds would appoint salaried medical officers "whose duty it shall be to supervise the sick and to decide when the insured shall receive the sick benefits, and when the sick are well enough to go back to work." If these referees—or the patient, the physician, or the directors of the insurance fund—desired a second opinion, they could refer patients to consultants, who in large towns and cities would commonly be associated with dispensaries. A state health insurance commission, appointed by the governor, would supervise this organization, assisted by

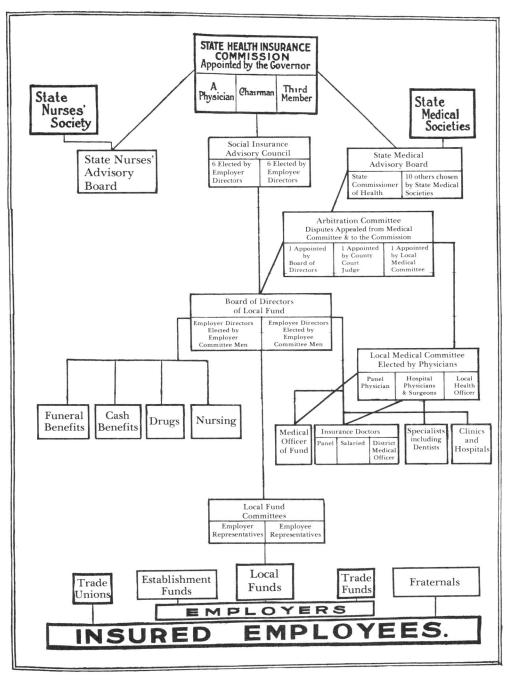

Fig. 12. The administration of compulsory health insurance proposed by the American Association for Labor Legislation (adapted from *Bulletin of the U.S. Dept. of Labor, Bureau of Labor Statistics,* #212, 1917, facing p. 646).

the state commissioner of health and a medical advisory board composed of representatives of the regular, homeopathic, and eclectic state medical societies. Such an arrangement, granting physicians adequate representation and freeing them from ruling on eligibility, would avoid "the quarrels and friction produced under the health insurance laws of the old world," said Lambert.[13]

In discussing this plan, several individuals questioned the likelihood of winning physician support. Emery R. Hayhurst, a leader in industrial hygiene and a staunch supporter of health insurance, estimated that eight of ten physicians—including both general practitioners and specialists—would oppose it; and others immediately challenged his figures for being too low. Representatives from both Ohio and Pennsylvania predicted stiff opposition in their states, in spite of the recent endorsement by the Medical Society of the State of Pennsylvania. The most optimistic assessment came from Frederick Green of the AMA, who said that "While it is probably true that a large per cent of the profession would to-day vote against the proposition, I do not believe that there is a single member of the medical profession who has given it careful and at all exhaustive study who is against it."[14]

In January 1917, *JAMA* published Lambert's address to the AALL together with a call for "constructive discussion of health insurance in the columns of THE JOURNAL."[15] The solicited reaction was mixed. On the negative side an Illinois physician, who acknowledged that Lambert was "probably the best informed man in the medical profession on this subject," professed having a difficult time understanding "the general tone of quiescent acceptance" on the part of American physicians. It was a mistake, he thought, to concede the inevitability of health insurance, when such a measure would only turn the physician from a trusted friend into a "salaried commercialist."[16] A Rochester practitioner wrote in to suggest paying workers a living wage rather than turning medicine into "a 40 cent profession commanding 30 cents' worth of respect," as had allegedly happened in England.[17] Similarly, a doctor from Buffalo predicted that health insurance would only "make matters worse by furnishing a heartless, overworked, 15-cent-a-call contract physician in place of a physician with a kind heart, who gladly donates his services to help humanity."[18]

Not all the respondents, however, feared compulsory health insurance. Arthur B. Emmons, 2d, a pioneer in social medicine and director of the Appointments Bureau at Harvard Medical School, expressed confidence that insurance would aid young physicians in setting up their practices and encourage them to organize into salaried groups.[19] S. S. Goldwater submitted fifteen reasons why he favored such legislation beginning with his belief that medicine "cannot rightfully be used for the exclusive benefit of the few."[20] And John Andrews, responding to insinuations that the AALL was exploiting the medical profession, said that "If the medical provisions of the bill, as now drafted, are unsatisfactory, it is because the profession has been slow in offering constructive suggestions."[21]

As these comments suggest, the most enthusiastic support for health insurance was coming from that segment of the medical profession that Rubinow called "institutional": "public health officers, hospital officials, and the teaching force of the larger medical schools."[22] Among the public health physicians who openly endorsed compulsory insurance were two presidents of the American Public Health Association, W. A. Evans and John F. Anderson; Rupert Blue, J. W. Schereschewsky, B. S. Warren, and Edgar Sydenstricker of the U. S. Public Health Service; Haven Emerson and Louis I. Harris of the New York City Department of Health; and others, like General W. C. Gorgas and Alice Hamilton, prominent in the field.[23] Delegates to the annual meeting of the American Public Health Association in 1916 were noticeably sympathetic to compulsory health insurance, and in May a conference of national and state public health officers unanimously passed a resolution "favoring the establishment of government systems of health insurance."[24] Additional support came from the *American Journal of Public Health*.[25] Public health physicians were, however, often reluctant to endorse the AALL's model bill. They wanted compulsory health insurance, to be sure, but only if it were to be an integral part of existing public health agencies.[26]

The most persistent advocate of this position was B. S. Warren, a surgeon in the U. S. Public Health Service and co-author with Edgar Sydenstricker of one of the earliest and most influential American studies of health insurance. To unite established health departments with the proposed health insurance system, Warren suggested simply amending the model bill so that the medical officers would be employees of the state rather than of the individual insurance carriers. A corps of salaried physicians and nurses employed by the department of health would supervise the local panels, and "no cash benefit [would] be paid except on the certificate of a medical referee appointed by such agencies." Not only would this plan avoid the friction that had developed in Europe between physicians and the insurance funds, it would encourage preventive medicine and "would prove to be the greatest public-health measure ever enacted."[27] Lambert readily conceded that Warren's proposal would indeed promote preventive medicine, but he doubted that the medical profession would like the idea of submitting to health department control.[28]

Among the well-known medical school professors who worked in behalf of compulsory health insurance were Lambert of Cornell, Richard Cabot and David Edsall of Harvard, Hayhurst of Ohio State, and E. P. Lyon of Minnesota.[29] While health insurance legislation would have had little effect on some of these men, the same was not true of the hospital superintendents who favored such action: Goldwater of Mount Sinai, Andrew R. Warner of Cleveland's Lakeside Hospital, and Thomas Howell of the New York Hospital, who also served as chairman of the American Hospital Association's Committee on Social Insurance.[30] Because the model bill included hospitalization, superintendents expected that their institutions would benefit financially by its passage.[31]

Sectarian physicians, principally the homeopaths and the eclectics, viewed the prospect of compulsory health insurance with concern. Above all, they feared that state insurance laws, framed with the assistance of the regular profession, would exclude them from panels and from representation on administrative bodies. Thus they insisted on open panels with free choice of physician.[32] Whatever their reservations, the homeopaths at their annual meeting in 1916 passed a resolution approving health insurance; and the chairman of the Committee on Social Insurance of the American Institute of Homeopathy, Hills Cole, explained that his committee had been formed expressly "to cooperate with the American Association for Labor Legislation in procuring the enactment of health insurance laws, such laws to be framed to reasonably conserve the interests of physicians in general and the members of our organization in particular."[33] The eclectics, however, refused to go along with their brethren, largely, it seems, because they feared that deleterious economic consequences might destroy an already suffering profession.[34]

The two paramedical professions most likely to be affected by health insurance, nursing and pharmacy, were also on opposite sides of the issue. In the spring of 1916 the three national bodies of nurses created a joint Committee on Health Insurance composed of Florence M. Johnson for the National League of Nursing Education, Mary Beard for the National Organization for Public Health Nursing, and Martha M. Russell for the American Nurses Association. At first the women were skeptical of compulsory health insurance, but the more they learned about it the more they became convinced of its potential benefits, and eventually, "to the surprise of all," they gave it a strong endorsement.[35] Two factors influenced their decision.

First, since the model bill specifically provided for nursing services, its passage promised to expand professional opportunities for nurses of all kinds: those on private duty, those in hospitals, and those working as visiting nurses. Once "the community learns the comfort of being *really nursed,"* predicted Miss Russell, the demand for nurses will increase.[36] The second factor influencing the nurses was their desire to share the benefits of health insurance, since many of them earned less than $100 a month. "We know of no group of people who are more entitled to such aid than nurses," declared the *American Journal of Nursing*.[37]

Druggists opposed insurance legislation for the understandable reason that it would undoubtedly reduce their business and compel them, as employers, to contribute to the insurance fund. Although the model bill provided for all necessary medicines, it did not specify how these would be supplied. Druggists, however, were sure that it would be through hospital dispensaries, even for home treatment; and this, they calculated, might reduce sales by 75 percent. By diverting the distribution of drugs to publicly supported dispensaries, health insurance might also force druggists to turn their shops into "general stores competing with other merchandising shops of which there are already far too many." In view of such dire consequences, the *Midland Druggist and Pharmaceutical Review* called compulsory health insurance the drug trade's "greatest menace." In 1917 the American Pharmaceutical Association established a committee on health insurance, not to study the matter objectively, but "to prepare arguments in opposition to Compulsory Health Insurance for presentation to state and local pharmaceutical associations, boards of pharmacy and other bodies opposed to such legislation."[38]

Outside the healing professions, social workers and social scientists were probably the most vocal advocates of compulsory health insurance. A survey of members of the National Conference of Charities and Correction and the American Economic Association revealed overwhelming support for social insurance, particularly health insurance. Of 675 respondents, 87 percent favored it, 9 percent were undecided, and only 4 percent opposed it. Significantly, 60 percent rated health insurance a more pressing need than either unemployment, old age, or widows' and orphans' insurance.[39]

In political circles compulsory health insurance won endorsements from prominent politicians of both major parties, including the governors of Massachusetts, New Hampshire, Wisconsin, California, and Nevada.[40] The small American Socialist Party, also provided strong support. When Meyer London was elected on the Socialist ticket to the House of Representatives in 1916, one of his first acts was to introduce a bill calling for the creation of a federal commission to investigate the need for health insurance. His bill was sent to the Committee on Labor, which held hearings for two days in April 1916. Among those appearing before the committee in behalf of London's bill were John Andrews, Joseph Chamberlain, Miles M. Dawson, and I. M. Rubinow, who appeared as the official representative of the Socialist Party. Federal legislation was preferable to state action, he explained, because of the time it took to get a bill through 48 different legislatures and because of the possible inequities that might result. Should it make a difference, he asked the congressmen, whether a person is hurt on the left or right bank of the Hudson River, in New York or in New Jersey? Despite his logic, the London bill fell 29 votes short of passage in the House, and subsequent attempts to revive it proved unsuccessful.[41]

The only witness to testify against London's resolution was Samuel Gompers, president of the American Federation of Labor, who argued eloquently that the solution to the problem of illness was not compulsory insurance but higher wages.[42] The argument that workers needed a paternal government because they were unable to provide for themselves repulsed the labor leader. "I am heart-sore, ill and sad when any, the least of my fellows, is hurt in any way," he said. "[But] sore and saddened as I am by the illness, I would rather see that go on for years and years, minimized and mitigated by the organized labor movement, than give up one jot of freedom of the workers to strive and struggle for their own emancipation through their own efforts."[43]

Gompers, of course, did not represent the entire labor movement. Even within the executive council of his own A. F. of L. he lacked the support of Vice President William Green and Secretary Frank Morrison on this issue, and in many states organized labor actively campaigned for compulsory health insurance.[44] It is also well to remember in evaluating the importance of Gompers' opposition that organized labor during the 1910s was hardly the powerful force it is today. In 1910 it embraced only 5.5 percent of industrial workers, and they were only a minority of America's labor force.[45] Nevertheless, the support of labor was crucial, if only for its symbolic value; and Gompers' intransigence had an inhibiting effect on many of his colleagues.[46]

By far the strongest opposition to compulsory health insurance came from the commercial insurance companies, which the AALL had deliberately excluded from serving as carriers. Their principal propaganda organization, the Detroit-based Insurance Economics Society of America, was created "to carry on necessary research work; to digest present systems of so-called

Social Insurance; to study proposed legislation dealing with Compulsory Health Insurance; to carry on a campaign of education, and to recommend practical and efficient methods for economizing present waste of time and human efficiency, and to thereby prevent needless suffering and hardship." Guiding the society's anti-insurance efforts were C. D. Babcock, secretary, and William Gale Curtis, chairman of the educational committee, who together during the course of the debate supervised the publication of at least a dozen *Bulletins* attacking compulsory health insurance.[47]

An occasional contributor to these *Bulletins* was Frederick Hoffman, Prudential statistician and late member of the AALL's Committee on Social Insurance. Since resigning from the committee, he had turned bitterly against his former colleagues, calling Andrews a liar and the Association's arguments for insurance "the most outrageous fabric of falsehood ever imposed upon the American public."[48] On one occasion he accused the AALL of deliberately misrepresenting the European experience with health insurance and of having "a total and wilful disregard of the results which are being achieved by voluntary and private effort," that is, by commercial insurance companies.[49] Though many suspected a connection between his rhetoric and his livelihood, Hoffman always denied that there were "business motives" behind his opposition to compulsory health insurance, which he believed was "more disinterested and more patriotic" than the AALL's position.[50]

Contrary to what the AALL claimed, he argued that most Americans were enjoying better health and better medical care than ever before. "I have the privilege of an intimate acquaintance with thousands of wage earners from Maine to California and from Minnesota to the Florida keys," he testified at the 1916 Conference on Social Insurance, and "my own investigations have conclusively shown that, broadly speaking, the needs of our wage earners, during even prolonged periods of sickness, are adequately met."[51] While some of his claims—for example, that the American death rate in 1915 was "the lowest on record"—were unquestionably true,[52] his sometimes intemperate attacks on compulsory health insurance stained his previously impeccable reputation for objectivity. According to AALL President Irving Fisher, many persons were beginning to think that they could no longer trust Hoffman "as a scientific man,"[53] and at times even Hoffman's friends were dismayed. H. E. Dearholt of Milwaukee, who respected the statistician for "having one of the most beautifully drilled, on the square, scientific brains" he had ever seen, admitted sadly that on the subject of health insurance "Hoffman's arguments and figures will not stand probing right down deep."[54]

Central to Hoffman's attack on compulsory health insurance was its alleged failure overseas, a point hotly contested by the AALL. In his opinion, the Association's claim that insurance had benefited both doctor and patient in Europe was based on a superficial investigation by Olga Halsey, and he thought it was simply "preposterous" that so much weight would be given to a hasty report by "some little girl." If nothing else, it proved that you could "flim-flam anybody if you have been to Germany."[55]

His own investigations of social insurance in Germany and Great Britain had shown it to be a dismal failure in every respect. It had not significantly reduced mortality in either country, but had only lowered the quality of medical service and the status of physicians.[56] His picture of life under National Insurance in England was so bleak, the *British Medical Journal* felt compelled to defend the Act. "His statement that insurance in England is a failure is certainly open to dispute," wrote an editor. "Even if it were admitted that the results have not reached expectations, it might still be argued that any such comparative failure arose from the insurance not going far enough, or from details in administration which experience will correct, and not from any defect necessarily inherent in compulsory health insurance."[57]

According to Hoffman, the most reliable study of European health insurance was that made in 1914 by a committee of the National Civic Federation.[58] This organization, founded in 1900 by newspaperman Ralph Easley, represented an effort "to bring together capitalists and labor leaders in a national forum." Its members included both labor leaders, like Gompers, and socially minded businessmen. Although the Federation had contributed to the passage of such progressive legislation as workmen's compensation, it remained unalterably opposed to any manifestation of socialism, which is how it viewed compulsory health insurance.[59] Ironically, Easley at first thought that health insurance was "mainly a scheme to promote the fortunes of the medical profession," while at the same time some physicians were blaming the agitation for health insurance on commercial insurance companies, which had close ties to the National Civic Federation.[60]

The Federation's initial survey of European health insurance plans was conducted in 1914 by J. W. Sullivan of the Typographical Union, Arthur Williams of the Association of Edison Illuminating Companies, and P. Tecumseh Sherman, a New York attorney. Following a visit to England during the summer they had concluded that the "greatest defect in the operations of the Act is the utter inadequacy and comparative inefficiency of the medical treatment provided." As they described it, English doctors did little more than "feel the patient's pulse, look at his tongue and prescribe for him some medicine to pour into this stomach." While professing to suspend judgment, the committee's report warned against "any spirit of impatience in America to copy these doubtful experiments."[61]

The appearance of the Federation's report at the very beginning of the campaign for compulsory health insurance brought an immediate response from AALL members, who tried their best to cast doubt on the study's reliability. Its distorted view of the British system, said Rubinow, stemmed from the fact that the report had only "one definite purpose in view—to discredit not only the English national insurance system but all compulsory social insurance as well."[62] Olga Halsey, who had personally investigated insurance in Great Britain, found the Federation's report marred by needless inaccuracies and a stridently hostile tone. While granting that the British system was not perfect, she nevertheless thought it was "most unfortunate that an early American study of the British situation should not have been based upon a more extensive investigation."[63]

The outbreak of war on the Continent had prevented the Federation committee from visiting Germany, but even without firsthand access to data Americans hotly debated the pros and cons of German health insurance. Critics attributed a reported 50 percent rise in absenteeism to malingering; defenders argued that the increase was "partly, if not wholly, due to improved and longer care of the sick."[64] Frederick Hoffman criticized the AALL for falsely claiming that insurance had markedly increased the life expectancy of Germans;[65] Rubinow in turn accused some Americans—meaning Hoffman—of rejecting even the most reliable of German statistics on the "convincing ground that the Germans believe in the Kaiser while we believe in the Declaration of Independence."[66] Such heated rhetoric tended only to confuse rather than clarify, but as America inexorably approached war with Germany the intensity of the debate increased manyfold.

6. ROUND TWO

The subject of Compulsory Health Insurance is the most important question
which the medical profession has had to face since the first white man set foot
upon the shores of North America and should be approached with a due consideration of the gravity and difficulty of the problem to be solved.

*Dr. Eden V. Delphey addressing the Medical Society
of the County of New York, January 1917*

The second round of the debate over compulsory health insurance
opened in an atmosphere pregnant with fear of impending war with
Germany, whose leaders warned the United States early in 1917 that they
would not longer respect the neutrality of American ships. Despite the
country's growing preoccupation with foreign relations, the AALL optimistically decided not only to continue its campaign for health insurance
but to expand it.[1] In January, when Senator Ogden Mills reintroduced the
revised model bill in the New York Senate, the state's physicians, unappeased
by their recently won concessions, reacted with unexpected bitterness.

Throughout the months of January and February county medical
societies across the state met in regular and emergency sessions to discuss
the Mills bill. Unlike the few such meetings the previous year, these were
marked by a distinct spirit of suspicion and urgency often mixed with overt
hostility. Leading the choir of critics, aroused by the prospect of a second
legislative battle and by the state Council's December 9 endorsement of the
model bill, was the Medical Society of the County of New York, which
scheduled a symposium on compulsory health insurance for January 22.

At the symposium it quickly became apparent that the Council's action
did not sit well with many of New York's practicing physicians. After listening
to four scheduled addresses on compulsory health insurance, the audience
launched into a lengthy and spirited debate over the wisdom and legality of
the Council's decision.[2] Samuel J. Kopetzky, the surgeon who had authored
the Council's resolution approving the Mills bill, defended his action as "a
step toward the mitigation of the present abuses of medical charity" and
predicted that "under the proposed bill the fees of medical men, both those
on the panels and those outside, would be increased."[3]

His promise of economic gain did not, however, sway the majority,

who seem to have been particularly upset by the Council's implied approval
of only "a reasonably free choice of physicians by the sick" and of salaried
doctors, paid by the insurance carriers, to supervise medical benefits. Shortly
after midnight they adopted a resolution, introduced by John P. Davin,
condemning the Council's endorsement on the grounds that in so doing it
"was usurping judicial and legislative functions not granted to it under the
Constitution and By-Laws of the Medical Society of the State of New York":

> Resolved, That the Medical Society of the County of New York disapprove
> and condemn this extra-legal, if not illegal, endorsement by the Council of the
> Medical Society of the State of New York of a measure not fully approved of by
> the body of the profession either in principle or in policy, while it is still under
> discussion by those most vitally affected by its provisions.[4]

But even this did not end the debate. Because of the lateness of the hour and
continuing disagreement, the meeting was adjourned until the evening of
February 14, when discussion would resume.[5]

In a marathon session that dragged into the morning hours of February
15, New York County physicians continued their deliberations.[6] Generally,
the doctors were divided into three camps. On the one hand were the
advocates of compulsory health insurance, men like Alexander Lambert,
S. S. Goldwater, I. M. Rubinow, and Kopetzky, who saw insurance as a
solution to the problem of inadequate medical care for America's working
classes. On the other hand were the intransigent opponents like Davin;
William S. Gottheil, a distinguished dermatologist; and Eden V. Delphey.
Both Gottheil and Delphey had previously professed open-mindedness on
the issue, but now Delphey was urging his colleagues not to be ashamed to
put their own financial interests ahead of society's alleged needs. He candidly
admitted "that a considerable part of his practice was among people who
would come under compulsory health insurance, and that he was fighting
for his own practice," since he probably could not afford to join a panel
for only $2,000 a year and consequently many of his patients would
abandon him for panel practitioners. Denying that American workers
even needed health insurance, Gottheil damned the Mills bill as a proposition that "would rob a hard-working and well-deserving body of citizens
[i.e. physicians] of a large part of their means of livelihood." In the middle
of these two groups were the physicians who freely admitted the desirability of compulsory health insurance but who objected to some specific
provisions of the Mills bill. In this camp were doctors like Edward D.
Fisher, chairman of the county society's Committee on Health Insurance;
Walter Lester Carr, another committee member; and Louis I. Harris, a

respected public health physician who saw health insurance as an inevitable step in man's struggle for freedom, "marked by the Magna Carta, the Cromwellian Revolt, the French Revolution, and the American Revolution."[7]

At the conclusion of the debate an exhausted society went into executive session to consider the following resolution from Delphey:

> Resolved, That this Society disapproves of the medical provisions of the bill for compulsory health insurance and the appointment of a legislative commission to study the subject, and directs its Committee on Legislation and the delegates of the Medical Society of the County of New York to the Medical Society of the State of New York to take proper measures to oppose its passage by the Legislature.

The motion passed, thus placing the largest and most influential of New York's county societies officially on record in opposition to the AALL's model bill, framed in part by two of the society's own members, Lambert and Goldwater.[8]

Before the vote Henry W. Berg had reminded the New York physicians that their action "was being watched by hesitating doctors all over this country who would be guided and influenced by the outcome of this meeting."[9] Undoubtedly he was correct, but upstate practitioners had certainly not been waiting in silence for their brethren in New York City to make a decision. Since the first of the year they, too, had been discussing and voting on compulsory health insurance, encouraged in many instances by James F. Rooney, an energetic Albany physician who served as chairman of the state medical society's Committee on Legislation and who used his position effectively to neutralize the influence of Kopetzky, the pro-insurance chairman of the Committee on Medical Economics.

On January 2 the Livingston County Medical Society voted its opposition to the Mills bill.[10] Two days later nine members of the tiny Washington County Medical Society, after communicating with Rooney both by letter and telephone, followed suit.[11] At a special meeting in the state capital on the 10th, attended by a number of visitors from neighboring Schenectady, Rooney's own Albany County Medical Society joined the opposition ranks, giving as its reasons that

> The proposed bill would be unfair to the individual laborer and to the plan of American liberty. It would force a form of socialism upon the people and at the same time be detrimental to the cause of organized labor. It appears to be unfair to the capitalist, and to be levying a double tax for the same purpose on land owners and rentpayers. It would create medical monopoly. And be conducive

to contract practice with its numerous vices and disadvantages. It places a legal limit to the number of patients which a physician may treat, and is dictating the amount of his fees and his income.[12]

Within a week the Schenectady physicians unanimously passed their own verbose resolution against compulsory health insurance and directed their secretary to send a copy of the minutes to all other county societies in the state.[13] Before the end of the month Rooney traveled west to Rochester to encourage the Monroe County Medical Society to express its disapproval of health insurance, which it did unanimously.[14]

The tide of opposition continued to swell during February and early March, with the medical societies of Chautauqua, Cayuga, Dutchess-Putnam, St. Lawrence, Richmond, Erie, and Kings County all voting against the passage of compulsory health insurance legislation.[15] Several of the societies also passed resolutions condemning the endorsement of the state Council, and the Chautauqua physicians even went one step further, voting to "instruct the delegates of our Co. Society to use every effort to prevent the election of Alexander Lambert to position as a member of the Council of the Medical Society of the State of New York."[16] If the attitude of Erie County physicians was typical, the source of this outpouring of antipathy was almost entirely economic in nature. New York practitioners had no desire, said one Buffalo doctor, to suffer the fate of physicians in England and Germany, "where the members of the medical profession were markedly reduced financially and many of them completely beggared."[17] Across the state H. G. Webster, editor of the *Long Island Medical Journal,* was driving home the same point. Adequate compensation for physicians, he said, was the one issue "that the medical profession must hammer at, must clamor for and must insist upon."[18]

About the only resistance to the current against compulsory health insurance came from the Broome County Medical Society. These physicians, convinced that unyielding opposition was futile, voted at a special meeting in Binghamton in January not to condemn health insurance but rather to insist that any legislation provide for adequate medical representation on supervisory bodies and for free choice of physician by patient.[19] But even the thoughtful doctors of Broome County could not resist for long; by March they were notifying other county societies that they, too, were now opposed to compulsory health insurance.[20]

In the face of such solid opposition and mounting criticism the state Council met in special session on March 3 and, at Rooney's insistence, rescinded its earlier endorsement of the Mills bill.[21] Thus by March 7, when the Senate Judiciary Committee opened hearings on the bill, the medical profession of New York had formed a virtually united front against the proposed legislation. The Lamberts and Goldwaters still remained hopeful, but they were now clearly out of step with the Rooney-led majority. When Goldwater pleaded at the hearings for the thousands who could not afford proper medical attention, the rhetoric of his opponents drowned his words. The Mills bill, declared Berg of New York City, was as "insane as anything that ever emanated from the wildest lunatic asylum in the country." It came, he reminded xenophobic senators, "straight from Germany" and was "devilish in principle and foreign to American ideals."[22]

John P. Davin, like Delphey a former pharmacist, was scarcely less intemperate in representing the Medical Society of the County of New York. Compulsory health insurance, he testified, was part of a vicious conspiracy, hatched by Abraham Flexner, "to uproot and destroy the traditional respect and confidence hitherto attached to the profession of medicine." It was unquestionably "the most ambitious medical proposition since Col. Sellers first offered his celebrated 'external, internal and eternal remedy for human ills.'"[23] The spokesman for the Erie County Medical Society, John D. Bonnar, continued the attack by denouncing the Mills bill as "an opprobrium"—a veritable marplot against liberty that would "place upon the shoulders of the medical profession the onerous duty of giving of their time, skill and intelligence, for a mere pittance, the needed medical, surgical and obstetric care for four-fifths of the population of the state." Obviously Mills' "monstrosity" had been conceived "in sin" and would, if enacted, be "brought forth in iniquity."[24] Duly impressed by the strength and animosity of his critics, Senator Mills once again backed down and reintroduced a substitute bill calling for the creation of a commission to study the need for health insurance. But even this attempted compromise apparently never got farther than the Finance Committee.[25]

At the annual meeting of the state medical society, held in Utica April 24-26, attention focused on compulsory health insurance and the ever widening gulf between Rooney's Committee on Legislation and Kopetzky's Committee on Medical Economics. In reporting to the House of Delegates, Rooney reminded his colleagues that he had been against compulsory health insurance since the very beginning, "in season and out of season." Partially because of his efforts, every county society that had taken action upon the Mills bill had opposed it, and Rooney was confident that the bill, which "embodies all the iniquities of both the German and English acts," would not pass the legislature during its 1917 session.[26]

Kopetzky, speaking for the Committee on Medical Economics, was especially anxious to explain the "great deal of misapprehension" that his recommendation to the Council had created. His committee, he argued disingenuously, had "never endorsed, never recommended for endorsement, nor even desired the unqualified endorsement of any part of Mills Bill No. 69"; it had merely approved the AALL's tentative draft. And no "particular harm" had been done, since the Council's action had in no way committed the state medical society to support the bill. On the contrary, great good had resulted: "we contend that the action of the committee and its approval by the Council at the meeting in December did more than anything else to focus concentration by our profession upon the proposed legislation, and we submit from observation upon the results obtained that as a matter of tactical strategy it was well and fully justified."[27] If nothing else, Kopetzky at least knew how to make the best of a very uncomfortable situation.

As he saw it, the physicians opposing compulsory health insurance could be divided into six categories: (1) the "honest objectors" who questioned the principles of health insurance; (2) those who feared importing the evils of foreign systems; (3) those with interests in private insurance companies; (4) those who feared a loss of income; (5) those who were unhappy with certain features of the proposed bill and damned the whole concept; and (6) "the great mass of the profession which is uninformed as to health insurance and opposes the measure for the time being in an effort to gain time to inform itself regarding it." Supporters fell into four groups: (1) the true believers; (2) those who saw it as a "measure involving intelligent communal philanthropy"; (3) those who believed it would "mitigate the evils of lodge practice, hospital and dispensary abuse"; and (4) those, evidently including himself,

who, whether personally favoring it or not, still do believe that it is the next step in social legislation in this state, and honestly think that sooner or later, and most likely sooner than it is realized, some form of this type of legislation will be enacted into law. They firmly hold to the belief that under these conditions and with this situation confronting the medical profession it were best to favor the proposed legislation, and to seek to so modify the medical provisions that the public welfare, the economic condition of the profession as well as the inherent interests of physicians in the maintenance of their high standards and in the advancement of preventive medicine — that all these be properly safeguarded under the proposed legislation.[28]

In concluding, Kopetzky recommended "that no action be taken at this time either for or against health insurance as a whole," but that his committee be empowered to continue working with the AALL to formulate legislation that would protect the interests of the medical profession. Furthermore, he requested approval for the AALL's medical provisions, worked out in collaboration with his committee, provided that "such approval should not be construed as approving any specific bill before the legislature." The delegates, however, were in no mood for such conciliatory gestures. Instead of approving Kopetzky's recommendations, they voted to express their opposition "to the present scheme of compulsory health insurance."[29] Later they removed Kopetzky as committee chairman and appointed in his place a declared opponent of health insurance, Henry Lyle Winter of Cornwall.[30]

Kopetzky's fall was not the beginning of a witch hunt. The same delegates who voted him out of office and rejected the Mills bill elected as their next president Alexander Lambert, who was probably more closely identified with health insurance than any other member. Ironically, the candidate he defeated, by a vote of 83 to 64, was James F. Rooney, the archcritic of insurance legislation.[31] Of late Lambert had been severely censured in some quarters for his stand on health insurance, but eleven years as treasurer of the state society had won him the respect and confidence of his colleagues. Some even appreciated his role in the insurance debate. The *New York State Journal of Medicine* that appeared the month of his election praised him (and Goldwater) for being "among the first to recognize the inadequacy" of the medical provisions of the AALL's tentative model bill.[32] And the chairman of the state medical society's Committee on Public Health and Medical Education acknowledged the constructive role Lambert had played in awakening the profession to the importance of health insurance.[33] But whatever Lambert's personal influence, it was not sufficient to convince the majority of New York physicians to follow him in supporting compulsory health insurance.

The second round of the Massachusetts debate over compulsory health insurance also began in January 1917, with the introduction of the so-called Young bill, a modification of the previous year's Doten bill.[34] In addition to guaranteeing open panels and free choice of physician by patient, the new bill provided for payment of physicians on a visitation rather than on a per capita basis and, unlike its predecessor, required that all salaried doctors compete equally with panel practitioners. "It is gratifying," ran an editorial in the *Boston Medical and Surgical Journal,* "that so much more detailed consideration has been given, in the Young bill, to the relationship of the medical profession to the proposed health insurance, than was apparent in the bill of last year."[35] In fact, the *Journal* was so appreciative, one reader accused it of "doing all it could to advance the 'Young' bill without coming out openly in its favor"—and this at the time of "the greatest crisis in our country's history, when our every effort and thought should be to our country's needs!"[36]

Additional support for compulsory health insurance came from a committee of over seventy distinguished individuals who organized a study group. Chaired by David L. Edsall of Harvard, the committee included laypersons like Mary Beard, Michael M. Davis, Jr., Carroll W. Doten, and Felix Frankfurter, and about two dozen physicians, drawn mostly from the Boston area. Among the physician members were Richard C. Cabot, Wade Wright, and Roger I. Lee. Wright and Lee, both of the Massachusetts General Hospital, had sponsored the Young bill; and although the Edsall committee professed not to be lobbying for immediate legislation, many of its individual members were."[37]

Massachusetts was, of course, not without its share of health insurance critics, especially in the Middlesex South District, where physicians in February voted unanimously against the Young bill.[38] It seems, quipped the president of the state medical society, that "the enthusiasm aroused in the Middlesex villages and farms by the ride of Paul Revere has not altogether subsided." Massachusetts physicians, asleep only a year ago, were now wide awake.[39]

In February the state society appointed a special Committee of 23 to investigate the need for compulsory health insurance. This group met once in March, but in June, following the outbreak of war with Germany, it requested that it be discharged and that no action on health insurance be taken for the duration of the hostilities:

In consequence of the entrance of the United States into the fearful European contest, medical men have been called upon as never before to consider questions relative to medical military preparedness and the care of our vast army and navy in action. So great has been this demand for medical officers for the war that it has been intimated in some quarters that there is a great possibility that there will be a shortage of medical men. Therefore it seems fitting that all those questions that do not clearly bear on medical military preparedness should be held in abeyance until after the war, and legislation that would apply to peace conditions would not apply to war conditions, or to conditions immediately after the close of the war. We would recommend that the Council oppose any comprehensive social insurance plan until after the war.[40]

The war thus effectively terminated the Massachusetts debate, but not before its influence had spread to other parts of New England, particularly

Rhode Island, where the medical profession applauded the concessions granted by the Young bill. In his 1917 presidential address to the Rhode Island Medical Society Edmund D. Chesebro noted approvingly that the medical profession seemed to be receiving "more liberal treatment" from the advocates of health insurance, even though many physicians remained prejudiced "because of the hardships imposed on English physicians." He himself favored a plan suggested by Frederic J. Cotton, the AALL's erstwhile ally in Boston, whereby medical treatment would be eliminated as an insurance benefit, leaving the insured to pay their doctors from their cash benefit. J. E. Mowry, chairman of the Committee on Social Insurance of the Rhode Island Medical Society, was also a partisan of this plan.[41]

Across the continent, in California, the Committee on Compulsory Health Insurance of the San Francisco County Medical Society endorsed the same idea. The San Francisco physicians felt that although most doctors would prefer to maintain the status quo, they would accept compulsory health insurance that provided only cash benefits.[42] Such limited insurance seems to have been equally acceptable to the Committee on Compulsory Health Insurance of the state medical society. Reporting in April, it endorsed "the principle of health insurance" but recommended that "at least until the war is over, and until more data on the subject are available, this Society should strenuously oppose all Health Insurance bills."[43]

In Wisconsin, where in 1916 the House of Delegates of the state medical society had unanimously embraced compulsory health insurance, the subject continued to attract considerable attention. County societies reported enthusiastic discussions, and at least one, the Rock County Medical Society, "went on record as opposed to compulsory health insurance."[44] In April the editor of the *Wisconsin Medical Journal,* L. M. Warfield, joined the critics of the 1916 endorsement with a warning against "going off half-cocked" in support of compulsory health insurance.[45] This advice provoked A. W. Gray, chairman of the Committee on Social Insurance, to reprove the editor for publishing a piece "so definitely antagonistic in spirit to the investigational work now being carried on by the Committee on Social Insurance" and for ignoring the committee's plea to "refrain from criticism and opposition not based on careful study." Since in all probability the legislature would not pass an insurance bill during the 1917 session, Gray thought there was ample time for deliberate discussion of the issues.[46] A chastened and apologetic Warfield affirmed his personal neutrality on insurance—"the most vital question which has ever touched the medical profession"[47]—but criticism of health insurance, partially stimulated by frequent contacts with neighboring Illinois, continued to grow in Wisconsin.

The physicians of Illinois, where no insurance bill had yet appeared, devoted more energy to combating compulsory health insurance than the doctors of any other state, except possibly New York. This is true in spite of the fact that most Illinois practitioners apparently did not care one way or the other about health insurance. When the chairman of the state medical society's Health Insurance Committee invited the county societies to share their views on the subject, only 16 or 17 of 101 even bothered to respond.[48] And in addition to these apathetic members, there were some who continued to believe that since compulsory health insurance was inevitable, unthinking resistance would prove to be self-defeating.[49]

Nevertheless, an influential minority of the state's physicians waged an all-out rhetorical war against insurance legislation. The acknowledged leader of the anti-insurance forces was Edward H. Ochsner, the Chicago surgeon, who opened the new year with an address before the North Side Branch of the Chicago Medical Society on "Some Objections to Health Insurance Legislation" and who probably did more than anyone else to convince Midwestern physicians that such legislation would be "a serious mistake."[50] As a member of the health insurance committees of the Chicago Medical Society and the Illinois State Medical Society, he played a crucial role in convincing both organizations that health insurance was unwise and un-needed. Prohibition, the Chicago committee contended, "will do away, in large measure, with the need, if any now exists, of health insurance, for the reason that after it is established people will have sufficient money with which to pay legitimate bills."[51]

At the annual meeting of the state medical society in May the Committee on Medical Legislation reported that it had been prepared to fight the insurance bill, but it never appeared. "We feel," said the chairman with a trace of pride, "that the active opposition of the medical profession prevented its introduction."[52] Before adjourning, the House of Delegates voted on the following resolutions, which were greeted with applause:

. . . Whereas, It is self-evident that the great rank and file of the physicians of Illinois and of the United States are opposed to health insurance . . . therefore, be it *Resolved,* That the House of Delegates of the Illinois State Medical Society instruct its delegates to the American Medical Association to introduce the following resolution in the House of Delegates of the American Medical Association:

Be It Resolved, That before proceeding further in this important subject, we recommend that the committee be asked to feel the pulse of the physicians of the United States, and in turn be guided by a popular opinion of the profession as to the desirability of compulsory health insurance;

   Be It Further Resolved, That, since the chief spokesman of the American Medical Association, Dr. Rubinow has made statements regarding the findings of the state commissions of both California and Massachusetts which are averse to the real facts, that in the future the committee be asked to censor his writings on the subject of health insurance before they are given publicity.[53]

   Elsewhere in the country, apathy generally prevailed. Sporadic interest was evident in places,[54] but most American physicians outside the major industrial centers remained serenely oblivious to the issues disturbing their colleagues elsewhere. Nevertheless, as the behavior of physicians in Illinois and New York illustrates, the AALL's brief honeymoon with the medical profession was fast coming to an end when the United States declared war on Germany in April 1917.

7. THE WAR

What is Compulsory Social Health Insurance? It is a dangerous device, invented in Germany, announced by the German Emperor from the throne in the same year he started plotting and preparing to conquer the world.

California League for the Conservation of Public Health, 1918

Whatever comes to us labeled "Approved in Germany" should be carefully examined beneath its wrappings to see if there be not concealed a Prussian.

Dr. George H. Coombs to the Maine Medical Association, 1918

In April 1917 the United States, angered by submarine attacks on American merchant vessels, declared war on Germany for the expressed purpose, as President Woodrow Wilson put it, of making the world safe for democracy. For the next year and a half, until the armistice of November 1918, the European conflict was "the one big question of the day." Thousands of patriotic American physicians—in some states as many as a fourth of the profession—temporarily abandoned their practices to "join the colors," leaving the debate over compulsory health insurance far behind them.[1] When Alexander Lambert, chairman of the AMA's Committee on Social Insurance, departed for France to serve as chief medical advisor to the American Red Cross, the committee closed down its New York office and its secretary, I. M. Rubinow, took a position as director of the Bureau of Social Statistics with the New York City Department of Public Charities.[2]

Of greater consequence to the health insurance debate was the indirect effect the war and related events had on attitudes toward social reform. Although the war was not solely responsible for turning the medical profession against compulsory health insurance, it unquestionably intensified the criticism already developing and further encouraged intemperate rhetorical attacks, based largely on the German origin of social insurance. For decades American physicians, thousands of whom had studied in German universities, had envied German culture, but as the war approached many of them began to realize "that there was much in German medical education that was undesirable from the American point of view, especially the disregard of patients, the neglect of ordinary students, and the lack of originality in much of their clinical work."[3] Many also disapproved of German imperialism in Asia, Latin America, and the South Pacific. Thus by early 1917 "the great majority of Americans" were already strongly anti-German.[4] In the outburst of patriotism that accompanied America's entry into World War I, this hostility turned into hysteria, in which Americans lashed out viciously against anything that smacked of Germany.[5] German-Americans were persecuted, the teaching of the German language was proscribed, and even the nascent psychoanalytic movement was nearly destroyed because of its Teutonic origin.[6] In deference to such feelings the proponents of compulsory health insurance began stressing its English rather than its German antecedents and making a point of always referring to it by the English name "health insurance" rather than by the German "sickness insurance."[7]

The medical profession was not immune to this wartime disorder. In his 1918 presidential address to the AMA, the distinguished Chicago surgeon Arthur Dean Bevan urged a nationwide witch hunt to seek out disloyal and unpatriotic members:

We as a profession must go into this war not only efficient, but we must go into it 100 per cent. loyal, 100 per cent. American. We are at war with a barbarous and brutal autocracy . . . . The Germans and Austrians who have chosen to make this country their home must choose between the land of their birth and America, the land in which their children are born . . . . there are a few [physicians] who are disloyal and would give aid and comfort to the enemy, and these must be sought out and interned where they can do no harm. It is the duty of every medical man and each county medical society to assist the government in securing the arrest and internment of every disloyal member of the medical profession.

Patriotic physicians, he continued, should report all German-American medical societies to the proper authorities and refuse to offer German doctors "the right hand of the fellowship of science until the German people drive from power and punish as they deserve the brutal and barbarous autocratic government."[8]

In April 1918 the Medical Society of the County of Kings (New York) not only voted 49 to 1 to drop James Peter Warbasse from the roster of members for writing a letter to the editor of the *Long Island Medical Journal* opposing the Chamberlain bill for compulsory universal military training after the war, but recommended that the United States District Attorney prosecute him. In the society's opinion, the Warbasse letter was "antagonistic to the welfare of the United States and the good repute of the Medical profession." In May the society reinstated him "under charges" but refused to let him explain his action or to accept his abject apology. "I wish unqualifiedly to recant and retract all statements in the letter," he wrote. "I realize now that the charges against me were properly founded and not in any sense animated by personal or professional reasons." Finally, six months after his ordeal began, the Council voted to readmit him to membership in good and regular standing since the adverse publicity had been "sufficient punishment." But the membership at large refused to support their action, leaving the Brooklyn doctor through the remainder of the war "a member of the Society under charges."[9]

As the war progressed, Americans in increasing numbers began referring to compulsory health insurance as "un-American" and predicting that it would lead to the "Prussianization of America." Many physicians came to regard the "health-insurance menace" as part of a Kaiser-inspired plot to spread German "Kultur" to the United States. "Whatever comes to us labeled 'Approved in Germany,'" warned a rural Maine practitioner, should be carefully examined beneath its wrappings to see if there be not concealed a Prussian."[10] The president of the American Surgical Association, Thomas W. Huntington, issued a similar warning: "With a clear understanding of German methods in molding public sentiment and with utter detestation of that sinister thing—German Kultur—we should hesitate long before subscribing to a dictum or a doctrine emanating from such a source." There was a real danger, he thought, that America might unwittingly be "making the world safe not only for Democracy but for Socialism."[11]

Widespread ignorance about the American sponsors of compulsory health insurance only fostered the view that it was a German conspiracy. This is illustrated by an incident that occurred during a Pennsylvania conference on health insurance. When one physician inquired as to who was back of the propaganda for insurance, no one was able (or willing) to give him an answer. The president of the state medical society said he was sure it was not the medical profession, since no one had "yet found a real, live, practicing medical man to speak a word in its behalf."[12] Another doctor said he had heard that "the real instigator of the subject came from New York City," but confessed that the true answer remained a "mystery" to him. F. L. Van Sickle, the author of the state society's 1916 resolution endorsing health insurance, was in the audience, but he apparently chose to keep discreetly silent.[13] In the absence of more certain information, it was easy to conclude that the American agitation for compulsory health insurance was indeed German inspired.

Persons familiar with the AALL's role in promoting health insurance legislation often portrayed its members as fifth columnists. "While President

Wilson is endeavoring to secure freedom and individual liberty to the peoples of the world," said one labor leader, "a small group at home is striving to do away with these rights and privileges which have made America the haven of the down-trodden."[14] A speaker at a well-attended meeting of the Milwaukee County Medical Society in Wisconsin attributed the health insurance agitation to a "little circle of the long-haired" trying to transplant German institutions to American soil.[15]

Even the federal government, in its eagerness to discredit all things German, turned against compulsory health insurance during the war. Opponents of the measure persuaded the powerful Creel Committee on Public Information, created in 1917 to "mobilize hatred against the enemy," to commission a series of articles exposing German social insurance as a fraud against the workers.[16] Supporters of health insurance protested that this was an unfair attempt to take "advantage of the state of the war existing between our government and Germany to prejudice people's minds against the movement in America for Health Insurance legislation," but their complaints apparently fell on deaf ears.[17]

The leading debunker of German health insurance continued to be Frederick Hoffman, the German-born life insurance statistician, who seemed driven to prove that he was a hundred-per-cent American—and who also seems to have collaborated with the Creel Committee.[18] It is only slightly hyperbolic to say, as John R. Commons told the Wisconsin State Medical Society, that all the anti-insurance literature "originates from one source; all of the ammunition, all of the facts and statistics that you may come across, no matter who gives them to you, will be found to go back to the Prudential Insurance Co. of America, and to Mr. Frederick L. Hoffman."[19] Hoffman's theme, expressed in the title of a widely circulated pamphlet, published shortly after the war's end, was the failure of German compulsory health insurance, failure to provide adequate medical care, to improve public health, and to support the medical profession. Instead, the system had only "fostered dishonesty, deception and dissimulation," traits that had become amply and disastrously evident during the war.[20]

Despite the war's overwhelmingly negative effect on the compulsory health insurance movement, a few significant gains were registered. As one commission noted, "Very soon it became apparent that the war, rather than furnishing a ground for the postponement of health insurance legislation, was, on the contrary, accentuating the need for it."[21] The passage shortly after the beginning of the war of the Military and Naval Insurance Act, entitling enlisted men to all necessary medical, surgical, and hospital services, set a precedent the AALL hoped the individual states might follow. After all, reasoned John Andrews, did not the "army of industrial workers" deserve equal consideration?[22] Also, the shock of having 29 percent of draftees rejected for being physically unfit convinced many citizens that American health care was not what it should be.[23]

Partially in response to the draft exemptions, as well as to sickness surveys showing the extent of illness among workers, labor unions during the war years began lining up behind compulsory health insurance. Early in 1918 the New York Federation of Labor, one of 25 labor organizations to endorse health insurance that year, became the tenth state federation to do so.[24] Additional support came from prominent Americans like Theodore Roosevelt and Senator Hiram Johnson of California, Roosevelt's running mate on the Progressive ticket in 1912. Addressing an audience in Portland, Maine, in March 1918, the former president called for enactment of health insurance legislation after the end of the war,[25] and Johnson a few months later cited social insurance as one of the "two outstanding progressive issues of the immediate future," the other being public ownership.[26]

During World War I the focus of the health insurance debate shifted from New York to California, where the legislature scheduled a referendum on the issue for November 1918, the only time voters in any state had an opportunity to express their wishes directly.[27] Thus while other Americans were allowing the war to eclipse health insurance, Californians were hotly debating the issue. Early in 1917 the state Social Insurance Commission, assisted the previous year by Rubinow, released its final report, recommending a system of compulsory health insurance for the state. To the disappointment of AALL leaders, however, the commission departed "from a fundamental of the standard bill of the Association" in preferring a state insurance fund over local mutual funds controlled by employers and employees. The commission also advocated separating the administration of cash and medical benefits and allowing the participation of voluntary insurance companies, which the AALL deemed very unwise.[28]

The medical profession of California remained divided on the issue, with many "high grade physicians" and public health doctors favoring health insurance and the more economically insecure general practitioners opposing it. At least this is how Rubinow interpreted the situation.[29] Organized medicine in the state remained surprisingly dispassionate, given the temper of the times. The Health Insurance Committee of the Los Angeles County Medical Society endorsed the major provisions of the model bill,[30] and the state medical society remained relatively neutral. In 1917 the House of

Delegates voted "that although such health insurance may quite possibly become highly desirable at some future day, for the present it is best to withhold legislation until such time as experience has proven the worth of social insurance as we now have it, and until political and economic affairs of our country have again become normal."[31] In view of the upcoming referendum, however, the Committee on Health Insurance, chaired by René Bine, continued to formulate medical provisions that would be acceptable to the medical profession.[32]

At the annual meeting of the state medical society in April 1918, President J. Henry Barbat, convinced that health insurance was imminent, urged California physicians to help frame legislation that would be fair to both workingmen and medical men.[33] By this time Bine's committee had worked out a list of demands, including free choice of physician, a minimum capitation of $5.00 a year, a maximum of 2,000 patients per physician, and free diagnostic centers staffed by salaried specialists in each medical district.[34] This proved to be too specific for the House of Delegates, which, instead of approving the committee's report, voted instead to ask the Council to "use every means within its power to secure such legislation as will best safeguard the interests of the medical profession."[35]

With the state society taking such a conciliatory position, a group of dissident physicians formed an independent California League for the Conservation of Public Health, whose primary object was the defeat of health insurance in November.[36] The League opposed insurance principally for economic reasons, fearing that it would "emasculate the medical, dental and pharmaceutical professions, and pauperize or bankrupt the members."[37] In its fight against compulsory health insurance the League constantly stressed the alleged connection with Germany. "What is Compulsory Social Health Insurance?" it asked in one of its tracts. The answer: "It is a dangerous device, invented in Germany, announced by the German Emperor from the throne the same year he started plotting and preparing to conquer the world." And "What are we fighting for 'Over There'? We are fighting for our American birthright—principles of equality and personal freedom—inalienable rights, that we must not forfeit here for this mess of German pottage—Compulsory Social Health Insurance."[38]

Outside the medical profession, commercial insurance companies and Christian Scientists mobilized the greatest opposition to compulsory health insurance. Representing the insurance industry in California was the California Research Society of Social Economics, a front organization for the Detroit-based Insurance Economics Society of America. Founded by

Carleton D. Babcock, the society consisted of little more than a well-financed speakers' bureau and a letterhead listing honorary officers. According to one of its employees, it neither conducted research nor studied economics, but simply engaged in propaganda and publicity. Among its publications, distributed by the thousands, was a pamphlet displaying a picture of the Kaiser over the caption: "Made in Germany. Do you want it in California?"[39]

Christian Scientists, though perhaps not so well financed, had the advantages of numbers. "Christian Scientists actually made it a religion to see that everyone had literature against the measure," reported one observer. "Every citizen received propaganda against the measure, not coming as an anonymous communication, but signed by some friend."[40] Because many of the governor's closest advisors were members of that denomination, it also enjoyed a disproportionate amount of political influence in the state.[41] In general, Christian Scientists opposed compulsory health insurance on the grounds that it interfered with their freedom of conscience and that it proposed "exclusively a material method of healing in preference to a spiritual method in which they believe." They naturally had no desire to subsidize a system that made no allowance for Christian Science practitioners.[42] California physicians, many of whom were wary of joining hands with a traditional enemy, charged Christian Scientists with being inconsistent. On one hand, they bitterly fought attempts at regulation or licensing, claiming that they were a religious body and did not practice medicine; on the other, they wanted their practitioners to receive compensation should health insurance legislation be enacted.[43]

On election day in November Californians went to the polls and soundly defeated the health insurance proposal by a vote of 358,324 to 133,858. While this massive repudiation of insurance represented a clear-cut victory for League physicians, insurance companies, and Christian Scientists, it was just as much the result of "apathy, unwillingness to add to taxation, the war, and the disposition on the part of the people to make no changes."[44] To a significant extent, compulsory health insurance was a victim of timing.

Elsewhere in the nation compulsory health insurance aroused comparatively little interest. For the third straight year the AALL in 1918 introduced its model bill in the New York legislature, even though this exposed them to the charge of "political trickery" for trying to push through the measure while so many physicians were off to war.[45] The 1918 bill, introduced by Ogden Mills' successor, Senator Courtlandt Nicoll, covered all employees regardless of their wages and limited cash benefits to $8.00 a week, changes made to win the support of the New York Federation of

Labor.[46] The new bill also incorporated most of the medical profession's demands: free choice of physician, the separation of medical supervision from the daily care of the sick, adequate representation on administrative bodies, and payment in proportion to services rendered.[47]

Nevertheless, New York doctors were still not satisfied, and Henry Lyle Winter, the new chairman of the Committee on Medical Economics, even claimed that the Nicoll bill "entirely ignores the medical profession."[48] County medical societies again voted their opposition, and in March a contingent of physicians, led by the indefatigable James F. Rooney, returned to Albany to testify against the bill before the Senate Judiciary Committee.[49] Once more they succeeded in killing the bill in committee. However, the state medical society still had not taken an official stand against health insurance, and at its annual session that spring Rooney pleaded with the House of Delegates to stop equivocating. "It is no longer possible for the Society to play hare and hounds with this question," he told them. "As a body it has given expression to no definite opinion; it is like a man trying to sit on two stools; the fall is inevitable as the position is prolonged."[50] Thus admonished, the delegates finally passed a resolution, submitted by the Committee on Medical Economics, disapproving of compulsory health insurance.[51]

In Massachusetts the Committee on Health Insurance of the state medical society reported little activity during the war.[52] Governor McCall continued to push for health insurance legislation,[53] but his efforts elicited scant response—perhaps because of the incongruity, as some saw it, of trying to fight the Kaiser and pass revolutionary legislation at the same time.[54] By 1918 most of the state's physicians seem to have decided against supporting compulsory health insurance. From Greenfield to the tip of the Cape, reported one knowledgeable observer, there was scarcely a doctor who favored it.[55]

Wisconsin physicians, whose representatives in 1916 had approved health insurance, grew increasingly uneasy during the war with this endorsement. In its annual report to the House of Delegates in 1917 the Committee on Social Insurance felt compelled to justify its continued support of insurance, and called on the profession to "stop fighting this at present formless thing called Compulsory Health Insurance unless we rescind our action in endorsing it in principle."[56] Throughout the next year while the committee was inactive, primarily because at least half of its members were in active military service, opposition continued to mount. In October 1918, A. W. Gray, chairman of the Committee on Social Insurance, noted the "unjustified feeling" against compulsory health insurance and warned the state medical society that "antagonism based on little understanding of the subject will work greatly to the detriment of the profession."[57]

By this time the committee, though still unanimous in its support of health insurance, was clearly embarrassed by the widening gulf between its position—ostensibly the position of the state society—and the attitude of many of the state's doctors, some of whom were deliberately undermining the committee's efforts. The committee was particularly incensed by the testimony of one society member at a hearing of the state legislature's Committee on Social Insurance. Allegedly the member had said "that there are only two doctors in the whole state of Wisconsin who are in favor of health insurance principles, and those are Gray and Dearholt, Gray, because he had only a silk stocking practice, and did not know anything about poor people, and Dearholt, because he saw in this another method of bringing more tuberculosis patients into the net."[58]

A similar ambivalence toward compulsory health insurance was evident within the AMA, whose official publication *JAMA* had become virtually silent on the issue. Before the Committee on Social Insurance had closed shop in May 1917 its secretary, Rubinow, had assisted in preparing a report for the annual AMA session in June, a document described by Morris Fishbein as a poorly concealed "plea for early adoption of compulsory sickness insurance in the United States."[59] Included in the report were two important resolutions. The first authorized the Council on Health and Public Instruction to continue studying health insurance and "to cooperate, when possible, in the molding of these laws that the health of the community may be properly safeguarded and the interests of the medical profession protected." The second, giving the AMA's four principles for acceptable compulsory health insurance legislation, instructed the Council "to insist that such legislation shall provide for freedom of choice of physician by the insured; payment of the physician in proportion to the amount of work done; the separation of the functions of medical official supervision from the function of a daily care of the sick, and adequate representation of the medical profession on the appropriate administrative bodies." The House of Delegates voted its approval and thus implicitly sanctioned the compulsory health insurance movement.[60]

But not all AMA leaders felt so progressively inclined. President Charles H. Mayo tried to straddle the fence, urging physicians to assist in "devising methods whereby the needy will receive aid [and] the middle classes will not be pauperized," while at the same time telling them to beware of "anything which reduced the income of the physician," since a lowered income "will limit his training, equipment and efficiency, and in the end will react on the people."[61] The Section on Preventive Medicine and Public Health, no doubt miffed by the AALL's refusal to place health insurance under the aegis of public health departments, denounced the "un-American" model bill as "a poorly conceived measure for poor relief, masquerading in the disguise of preventive medicine," and resolved "to oppose the scheme for compulsory health insurance in every way possible."[62]

Even Frederick Green, once the AMA's most ardent advocate of health insurance, began during the war to waver in the face of growing opposition and on one occasion flatly denied that he had ever endorsed the measure. Responding to a letter that had listed him among physicians who had "declared themselves in favor of Health Insurance," he wrote:

Regarding my personal attitude . . . I can only say that I have never made any such statement, either publicly or privately. The only statement which I recall that could possibly be so construed was made at the annual meeting of the American Association for Labor Legislation in Columbus last fall. In the discussion of Dr. Lambert's paper, I emphasized the importance of the problem and the need of careful study of it and urged that time be given for the education of the medical profession, adding, as I remember, that I did not know of any physician who had given the question careful study who was opposed to health insurance. I doubt whether this statement would hold good at present.[63]

In view of his past correspondence with the AALL, it is difficult to escape concluding that Green was merely an opportunist, willing to sell his endorsement to the highest bidder. Nevertheless, his defection was a severe blow to the health insurance movement and scarcely augured well for its future success.

8. THE FINAL ROUNDS

Compulsory Health Insurance is an Un-American, Unsafe, Uneconomic, Unscientific, Unfair and Unscrupulous type of Legislation [supported by] Paid Professional Philanthropists, busybody Social Workers, Misguided Clergymen and Hysterical women.

> *Dr. John J. A. O'Reilly to the Medical Society*
> *of the County of Kings, New York, October 21, 1919*

If you boil this health insurance matter down, it seems to be a question of the remuneration of the doctor. Now, that may sound harsh, but it is a statement which I think represents the real situation.

> *Dr. George W. Kosmak to the Medical Society*
> *of the County of Kings, New York, October 21, 1919*

In November 1918 the Great War ended and Americans, yearning for "normalcy," turned their attention from foreign enemies to problems within. The AALL, still hoping for victory in at least a few states, began preparing for its fourth annual campaign on behalf of compulsory health insurance. Following their crushing popular defeat in California, the reformers once again concentrated their efforts on New York, where success seemed most likely. In addition to the enthusiastic backing of the New York State Federation of Labor, they now had the support of such organizations as the City Club of New York, the State Woman Suffrage Party, the Consumers' League, and the Maternity Center Association.[1] And for the first time in New York the governor's office was on their side. In his inaugural message on January 1, 1919, Governor Alfred E. Smith "strongly" urged the enactment of a health insurance law to reduce poverty and disease.[2]

The 1919 New York campaign got off to a false start, as far as the AALL was concerned, when a state senator on New Year's Day introduced a "fake" insurance bill, Senate Bill No. 1, prepared by the Associated Manufacturers and Merchants of New York State, which opposed compulsory health insurance.[3] Two weeks later, however, Senator Frederick M. Davenport, a progressive Republican "regarded by many as the ablest man in the Senate," and Assemblyman Charles D. Donohue, the Democratic minority leader, co-sponsored the "genuine" AALL-approved legislation, providing strong bipartisan support in the Republican-controlled legislature.[4]

At the urging of President Thomas H. Halsted of the New York State Medical Society, the county societies reaffirmed their opposition to compulsory health insurance and wired their respective legislators to oppose the

Davenport-Donohue bill.[5] Some physicians, including those in Erie and Rensselaer counties, even pledged to boycott the law if it should pass. "Because of our unalterable convictions and firm belief in the ultimate destructiveness of the proposed method of practice to the interests of the public, we do mutually and severally agree that we will not engage in the practice of medicine under the proposed legislative enactment, or any similar enactment, that may hereafter be proposed," declared the Buffalo doctors. "We do this because we are convinced from our experience and knowledge of the working of compulsory health insurance in foreign countries that this manner of practicing medicine will not secure good services for the sick or injured."[6]

Other county societies adopted a more conciliatory approach, with some even recommending amendments to the bill that would make it at least tolerable, if not desirable. The physicians of Ithaca (Tompkins County), who had no objection to the principle of compulsory health insurance, suggested a statewide panel of practitioners, the inclusion of all employees earning under $50 a month, a minimum fee per visit, and free choice of physician.[7] On February 24, over the protests of John P. Davin, who wanted to "repudiate compulsory health insurance, root and branch, body and soul," the New York County Medical Society approved a similar set of amendments, prepared by a special committee headed by Eden V. Delphey.[8] That same evening the medical society of neighboring Kings County sponsored a mass meeting on insurance that attracted 450 Brooklyn doctors, dentists, pharmacists, and optometrists. Among the demands agreed upon by this group was the right of district physicians to set their own minimum fees.[9]

From this meeting grew the Professional Guild of Kings County, an organization of doctors, dentists, and druggists dedicated to protecting the economic interests of the professions most likely to be affected by health insurance. Leaving scientific matters to the gentlemanly state and county societies, the Guild sought freedom to threaten "an individual legislator with political annihilation" if he supported "such pernicious, humiliating, degrading, confiscatory, uneconomic, wasteful and un-American legislation as the Davenport-Donohue Health Insurance Bills and the like."[10] Among the Guild's leaders were H. G. Webster, the formerly pro-insurance editor of the *Long Island Medical Journal,* and John J. A. O'Reilly, a lawyer-physician who had recently returned to his native Brooklyn from Sullivan County, where he had been associated with the Loomis Sanitarium.[11] This fiery and bombastic doctor, who was to become so visible in the last phases of the health insurance debate, had obtained his medical degree in 1901 from the Long Island College Hospital, studied law at the Brooklyn Law School and St. Lawrence University, and joined the New York bar in 1909. Since 1913 he had lectured on legal medicine at the Brooklyn Law School, and since 1919, had edited a column on legal medicine for the *International Journal of Surgery.*[12]

O'Reilly was a born propagandist, and he unstintingly gave his talents to the cause of defeating compulsory health insurance. In a Guild pamphlet denouncing the Davenport-Donohue bill, he lashed out in his inimitably vitriolic style at its advocates:

Behind this Bill is an organization called the American Association for Labor Legislation, MADE IN GERMANY as part of the Infamous Kultur and imported to this Country by a Russian disciple of Bolshevism and I WON'T WORKISM; its Board of Officers contain the names of Hysterical men and women and vicious men and women who have no knowledge of or sympathy with the needs of working people and who believe that the working man does not know what is good for him and THEY DO and they are willing to take lucrative positions under the Davenport-Donohue Bill to do him good and to DO HIM —good; these people are Paid Professional Philanthropists, and busy-body Social Workers . . . Supporters, Defenders, Associates of the Forces of unrest known as the I.W.W. and Bolshevists; the disciples of Lenin and Trotzky whose Gospel is the Destruction of those things worth while for which men and women have given their lives.[13]

Such unrestrained language, identifying the AALL with Germans, Bolsheviks, and labor radicals, revealed not only O'Reilly's hostilities but the country's growing and often irrational fear of unrest during the postwar period. During the early days of World War I American hatred had centered almost exclusively on things German, but following the October Revolution in Russia and especially after the signing of the Russian-German armistice, American writers carelessly and indiscriminately lumped Bolsheviks together with other "German agents" like the Industrial Workers of the World, a much-feared labor organization. The nation's obsession with Bolshevism increased in 1918 and 1919 with the United States' intervention in Russia and then "froze into bitter, often bizarre, hostility." "It was," says Peter G. Filene, "as if the emotions of the war crusade, not yet satisfied, frantically sought new objects."[14]

Domestic events further increased fears of radicalism. Rampant postwar inflation drove millions of workers to the picket lines and impelled a handful to acts of terrorism, producing the notorious Red Scare. Many Americans, convinced that a radical revolution was in the making, succumbed to hysteria and paranoia. By late 1919, writes one historian, "a radical was anyone suspected of being pro-German, a Russian or other foreigner, a person who sent bombs through the mails, a believer in free love, a member of the IWW, a Socialist, a Bolshevist, an anarchist, a member of a labor union . . .or anyone who did not particularly agree with you."[15]

In such a superheated atmosphere compulsory health insurance and its advocates could scarcely escape unsinged. In a widely reprinted essay entitled "A Bolshevik Bolus" a New York dermatologist accused his pro-insurance colleagues of being crypto-Bolsheviks. "With your eyes shut you could not distinguish in the smooth utterances of Lambert, or Goldwater, and the raucous ravings of the Russian Reds any essential difference," he wrote. "They are for the socializing of medicine!" In his opinion, socialism would be "as firmly established by compulsory health insurance as it would be by the acceptance of the whole Marxian system," and the only solution was to bolt "the whole loathsome Bolshevik Bolus."[16]

The fact that some prominent proponents of compulsory health insurance, like Rubinow, were known Socialists did not help. When J. P. Warbasse, the ostracized Brooklyn physician, criticized the medical profession for its attachment to "property, precedents, and the old order of things" and called for an end to individualistic competition, he was branded a Bolshevik.[17] The Associated Physicians of Long Island demanded an end to such "radical socialism,"[18] and an obviously anti-Semitic New York City practitioner denounced "those foreign born elements in our body politic who are not in sympathy with our ideals, religion, or institutions, and whose incapacity has resulted from sexual license, hereditary animosities, and racial and religious hatred." Warbasse's arguments had insulted the physician's "Anglo-Saxon intelligence," and he wanted no more of "this sort of socialistic bunk" from that "apostate German Jew," Karl Marx.[19]

Some backers of compulsory health insurance attempted to defuse the Red issue by claiming that insurance against sickness would actually serve as a bulwark against Bolshevism. Introducing himself as "an anti-Bolshevist liberal of the Roosevelt style," Senator Davenport told the Medical Society of the State of New York that the best way to deal with the menace from Moscow was to do "away with the sources that gave rise to Bolshevism by trying to make this world a better and a happier place in which to live." A "great, strong, contented working class," he thought, would serve as "the best barrier to Bolshevism"; and American workers wanted compulsory health insurance.[20]

During February and March AALL officers, eager to win the support of the medical profession, met with a committee of representative physicians to work out remaining differences. According to J. B. Andrews' reckoning, the model bill by mid-March had incorporated 14½ of the physicians' 16 demands.[21] These included the abolition of local panels in favor of a statewide panel of doctors, the creation of medical advisory committees at both state and local levels, the mandatory appointment of a physician as head of the Health Insurance Bureau, the establishment by the State Industrial Commission of fee schedules that varied from community to community (with the possibility of appeal), and a prohibition on contracts between local funds and physicians.[22] Still, the doctors were not satisfied. They wanted an absolute ban on contracts with individual physicians, including arrangements between the Industrial Commission and local doctors; and they wanted to have a greater voice in setting fees.[23] Their failure to win these two vital concessions led some to accuse the AALL of not bargaining in good faith, which in turn prompted one disgusted AALL lobbyist to recommend forgetting about the doctors and letting them "hang themselves."[24]

Both sides of the debate agreed on one point: the medical profession's chief objection to compulsory health insurance was monetary. To identify a doctor in any New York crowd, went one joke, all a person needed to do was "to whisper 'health insurance' in a man's ear and see whether his hand instinctively goes to his pocket."[25] As a somewhat exasperated John Andrews saw it, the "crux of the whole problem" was that physicians were constantly hearing the deliberate lie that the model bill would limit them to 25 cents a visit or about $1,200 a year.[26] "If you boil this health insurance matter down, it seems to be a question of the remuneration of the doctor," observed George W. Kosmak of New York City, who believed that 99 out of a 100 physicians had taken up the practice of medicine primarily "as a means of earning a livelihood."[27] Another New York City practitioner, who opposed the Davenport-Donohue bill, described all other objections besides remuneration as "merely camouflage for this one crucial thought." Medical opposition would melt away, he predicted, if adequate compensation were guaranteed.[28]

Considerable evidence supports this view. Not only did physicians demand a decent income as a condition for working under health insurance, but some of them freely admitted that they would prefer a comfortable salary to the uncertainty of a fee-for-service practice. According to one report, most New York physicians envied the laboratory man at the Rockefeller Institute, "because he receives a salary-check at the end of the month."[29] A president of the New York State Medical Society (1919-20), Grant C. Madill, thought that a "fixed salary for a medical man would be a blessing," since doctors were such notoriously poor businessmen. The experience of research physicians, doctors in the armed forces, and medical school professors proved, he said, that no initiative was lost "by having an annual salary and the moral support of an established institution."[30]

On March 19 an overflow crowd jammed the Assembly chamber in Albany to witness the joint Judiciary Committee hearings on the Davenport-Donohue bill. Testifying for the measure were representatives of various women's, civic, and labor organizations, as well as an occasional employer or physician. Opposing it were manufacturers and merchants, Christian Scientists, and the preponderance of physicians, nearly 400 of whom were in attendance. Kings County alone sent almost 50, and scarcely a county society was unrepresented.[31] By this time most of the state's 15,000 physicians —perhaps over 95 percent—wanted nothing to do with health insurance, no matter how many compromises were offered.[32] "The Bill," declared Thomas H. Halsted, president of the state medical society, "would, if enacted, bring about a demoralization and degradation of the medical profession, and an interruption to the progress of medicine that was simply appalling."[33]

Both Alexander Lambert and Louis I. Harris, of the New York City Health Department, spoke in favor of the bill, but Lambert was apparently the "only physician in private practice" to do so.[34] The officers of the state medical society, including President Halsted, Vice President James F. Rooney, and Henry Lyle Winter, chairman of the Committee on Medical Economics, all testified against the measure,[35] as did old Dr. Delphey, a "Johnny-on-the-spot" at such occasions, whose speech this time was uncharacteristically "mild and largely ineffective."[36] Rooney, who concluded the medical testimony with an "impassioned plea against paternalism," was clearly the opposition leader. He is "some fighter," reported Andrews with a trace of admiration—"tricky, eloquent, and possessed of an undying ambition to ride into the office of president of the State Medical Society on his opposition to health insurance. Reasonable arguments, therefore, do not appeal to him."[37] As Rooney explained to an assemblyman, the medical profession objected to the Davenport-Donohue bill for two reasons: "*First,* on the broad grounds of public policy with the complete understanding that this is one of the measures of the Prussianization of America; *Secondly,* that it is a social goldbrick which is very apparent to anyone who will study the question of its effect in Germany and in England."[38]

Immediately after the hearings Senator Davenport began holding private conferences with physicians and other opponents of his bill to work out additional compromises, which he introduced as amendments on April 1. For the doctors, he agreed to grant county medical societies the right to propose fee schedules. For employers, he agreed to drop dependents from health insurance coverage and to allow company insurance plans to continue operating. For Christian Scientists, he agreed to a conscientious objector's clause, allowing "persons who are members of an existing religious sect whose tenets preclude the practice of medicine" to be exempt. Finally, on April 10, in hopes of winning a few more crucial votes, he made one more concession, exempting employers with fewer than eight employees from participating in the plan.[39] Surely now, thought Andrews, "all reasonable objections of doctors, employers, Christian Scientists and others have been met."[40]

April 10, 1919, marked the "high point" of the American debate over compulsory health insurance. On that day the New York Senate became the first legislative body in the United States to endorse the measure. After an all-day debate, punctuated with acrimony, nine "insurgent" Republicans broke with their party leadership to join 21 Democrats in voting 30 to 20 for passage.[41] But the taste of victory was short-lived. Assembly Speaker Thaddeus C. Sweet, a conservative Republican manufacturer, vowed that he would never let the health insurance bill and other welfare measures out of committee for a vote on the Assembly floor. Despite a public outcry against Sweet's tactics, Assemblyman Donohue's motion on April 17 to discharge the Judiciary Committee of his bill lost by a vote of 84 to 58.[42] That same day Governor Smith, convinced that Sweet "could not be budged from his opposition," reluctantly admitted defeat, dashing the AALL's hopes for the first enactment of their bill.[43]

The defeat, attributable in part to one man's intransigence, demonstrated to physicians the power of a united profession. To Andrews, it indicated the need for greater "education" in the industrial centers of upstate New York, like Buffalo, Rochester, Syracuse, and Utica, where opposition was particularly strong.[44] In Utica, for example, a poll of 13,000 factory workers following an anti-insurance campaign showed 12,875 opposed to compulsory health insurance and only 112 for it, an obvious embarrassment to an association that claimed to represent the working class.[45]

The Albany setback also suggested that, contrary to popular belief, compulsory health insurance was not inevitable. One county medical society now concluded—not without justification—that "90% of the 'inevitability' talk can be traced directly to Mr. Andrews and a few other propagandists."[46] At the annual meeting of the state medical society in May Rooney made the same point, telling the delegates that the myth of inevitability was nothing but subtle propaganda, like that used by Germany during the war, designed "to undermine the morale of opponents by creating the psychological attitude of defeat." The myth could not long survive, he thought, in the face of the current "reaction against all forms of socialism and communism."[47]

Unlike many delegates who opposed the Davenport-Donohue bill but nevertheless maintained "a constructive, conciliatory attitude" toward compulsory health insurance, Rooney urged "no compromise" at all.[48] To some, like John P. Davin, a long-time foe of insurance, this made him the "logical candidate for president of the Medical Society of the State of New York,"[49] but the majority voted instead for the less outspoken Grant C. Madill of Ogdensburg, who defeated Rooney by a vote of 80 to 61.[50] (Two years later, however, Rooney finally won the much-coveted office.)

Another sign of continuing openmindedness was the president's controversial invitation to Senator Davenport to address the delegates on the subject of compulsory health insurance.[51] At least some of the state's physicians admired the senator for his courtesy to the medical profession and for his willingness to entertain constructive criticism.[52] In response to his request for suggestions from physicians, the Erie County Medical Society had even proposed as an alternative to compulsory health insurance the establishment of government-financed "group diagnostic clinics" that would be available to all licensed physicians.[53] The Committee on Economics of the state medical society and at least one other county society subsequently endorsed the plan,[54] but most physicians bitterly denounced Erie County's so-called "compromise."[55]

Among the critics were a number of Buffalo doctors who felt that their medical society "lacked the vision, the capacity, and the agressiveness" to effectively combat the threat of health insurance. During the summer they organized a Physicians' Protective Association, modeled after the Professional Guild of Kings County, for the expressed purpose "of fighting compulsory health insurance and killing it." Membership cost $10, but even so the Association within thirty days had signed up 450 of the county's 550 practitioners; and the movement was spreading "like wildfire through the western half of New York State."[56]

A major confrontation between compromisers and noncompromisers on health insurance took place in Brooklyn on the evening of October 21 at a symposium sponsored by the Kings County Medical Society. Three of the five speakers—Lambert, Madill, and Kosmak—favored continuing discussions with the AALL, if only to protect the interests of the medical profession. The "present foolish ostrich-like attitude of refusing even to discuss health insurance" is dangerous, warned Lambert. "Thrusting the head in the sands of prejudice leaves the flanks exposed and renders the position both vulnerable and speedily untenable."[57]

This advice was quickly forgotten when John J. A. O'Reilly, the firebrand from the Professional Guild, arose to deliver his maiden address against compulsory health insurance. Added to the program at the last minute in the interest of "fair play," he took the opportunity, as he described it, to call "spades—spades and [to define] treachery in high places." *"Compulsory Health Insurance,"* he began in characteristically purple prose,

is an Un-American, Unsafe, Uneconomic, Unscientific, Unfair and Unscrupulous type of Legislation equalled only in viciousness and cowardice and contemptibility by the so-called Contraceptive Bill whose advocates and supporters were found to be the same group of Paid Professional Philanthropists, busybody Social Workers, Misguided Clergymen and Hysterical women (none of them with knowledge of or sympathy with the needs of the working people) who urge the enactment of the Davenport-Donohue Compulsory Health Insurance Bill.

Then specifically addressing the three speakers who had preceded him, he continued his alliterative attack:

You are charged with knowledge that Compulsory Health Insurance is a debasing, wasteful, vicious plan; a Legislative Monkey Wrench which is to be cast into the Machinery of Society without regard to *any result* save that some politicians and some professional Philanthropists and Sociologists may get some jobs. . . . You know or *should know* that the Penalization of *Panelization* is the Prostitution of your Profession, the Pauperization of the People and the Profiteering of the Politician.

Before taking his seat, O'Reilly introduced a resolution reaffirming the society's "uncompromising opposition to the Davenport-Donohue Compulsory Health Insurance bill," and demanding a popular referendum on the issue. The Brooklyn physicians, swayed by this dazzling rhetorical display, voted their approval.[58]

In November, for the second time in two years, the House of Delegates of the New York State Medical Society finally voted its opposition to compulsory health insurance. The occasion for this action was an "unprecedented special meeting called by the president for November 22. According to the secretary of the society, nothing since the Code of Ethics debates in the 1880s (which resulted in New York's temporary expulsion from the AMA) had "aroused so much interest or generated such diverse opinions and intense feeling."[59] As the special session approached, some county societies passed resolutions instructing their delegates to vote against health insurance or any substitute measure.[60] The physicians of Oswego County, however, detected a danger greater even than social insurance: the possibility of a schism within the state society brought on by the outbursts of anti-insurance doctors. Four days before the House of Delegates convened, they passed a motion deprecating "the critical spirit of some" and deploring "any act which might lessen the cohesion of its parts or lower the standards of dignity in the Medical Society of the State of New York."[61]

The central event of the November 22 meeting was the report of a special nineteen-man committee on compulsory health insurance under the chairmanship of Harvey R. Gaylord of Buffalo, author of the Erie County compromise. Among the other members were Madill, Halsted, Winter, Rooney, Kosmak, Albert T. Lytle of Buffalo, J. Richard Kevin of Brooklyn, and S. S. Goldwater, a last-minute addition. When the group had met in late July, fifteen of its members had agreed on a list of essential principles, including free choice of physician, payment on a fee-for-service rather than a capitation basis, the exclusion of commercial insurance companies, a limit of 500 insured families per physician, and more than a dozen additional demands. By November, however, the committee, perhaps pressured by the county societies, had reversed itself, and seventeen of its members—all but Goldwater and Kosmak, who abstained—submitted the following negative report:

First, that there is no necessity for social insurance in New York; second, that in those countries where it has been in operation for many years, it has caused a deterioration in medical morale and medical service, and that it would have the same effect in New York; third, that in comparison with those countries where social insurance has been in operation, the United States has shown a more marked reduction in both mortality and morbidity; fourth, that there is danger of social insurance, if adopted, gradually undermining the extremely valuable functions of the state department of health; fifth, that owing to the paucity of accurate and unimpeachable data, the committee recommends that the legislature of 1920 be requested to appropriate enough money for a survey of the amount and character of illness in the State of New York and its economic relation to the commonwealth; sixth, that if additional legislation is to be enacted at present, it should provide for a greater development of preventive medicine . . . . Your committee, therefore, recommends that the House of Delegates,

and, through them, the Medical Society of the State of New York, unqualifiedly
oppose the enactment by the Legislature of the State of New York of any law
instituting a system of compulsory insurance against sickness, because of its
menace to the public health of the State.

The House of Delegates voted its unanimous approval.[62] Although Goldwater
had prepared a minority report, consisting mainly of the principles the
majority had adopted in late July, the delegates, through what Lambert
called "one of the most incomprehensible bits of poor management," were
never officially given his statement.[63] Prospects for compulsory health
insurance, so bright for a few days in April, now seemed dimmer than ever.

During late 1919 and early 1920 the hysterical Great Red Scare reached
its peak, making the passage of social welfare legislation even more unlikely.
On November 7 Attorney General A. Mitchell Palmer launched his notorious
raids with the arrest of hundreds of suspected Communist aliens, 249 of
whom were deported, presumably to Russia, on the "Soviet Ark." On January
2 the government seized thousands of radicals in cities across the country,
and five days later Speaker Sweet accused the five Socialist members of the
New York Assembly with disloyalty and denied them their seats.[64] "Everything is in a very reactionary state in this country now," wrote Andrews to
Rubinow in a letter telling him of the expulsion of his "five Socialist brothers"
from the Assembly.[65] Rubinow, who had been in Palestine for almost a year
organizing the Zionist Medical Unit and applying his "principles of socialized
medicine," replied that he "should like to visit Russia but [did not] enjoy the
prospect of being deported there, thank you."[66]

Despite the country's sullen mood, Andrews decided in 1920 to try one
last time to get the AALL's much-revised and much-misunderstood model
bill through the New York legislature. On March 11 Senator Davenport
reintroduced his bill, prompting the editor of the *Long Island Medical
Journal* to note the "particularly grim sort of humor in the situation when
one considers the possible acceptance of practical Socialism of this type by
a State Legislature that has just ousted five Socialists."[67] Because "public
opinion had been poisoned against it," even Davenport gave his bill little
chance of passing.[68] Nevertheless, the Senate Labor and Industrial Committee
held hearings in April, and many familiar faces came back to testify.[69]
Lambert, however, stayed away this time. In 1918 he had been elected
president of the AMA, and since the Association had not yet taken a
stand on compulsory health insurance, he felt that there was "a grave
question" whether he should again testify for the bill.[70] Abandoned by its
most effective apologist, the bill apparently died in committee.

Meanwhile, compulsory health insurance had acquired a new and dangerous enemy, the New York League for Americanism, a "camouflage" for the commercial insurance companies. Heading the organization was Carleton D. Babcock, a representative of the Insurance Economics Society and the same man who had directed the California Research Society of Social Economics during the California campaign of 1918.[71] Apparently Babcock was collaborating with the anti-insurance doctors in Buffalo; the president of the Medical Society of the County of Erie, who was also secretary of the Physician's Protective Association, had the same address as the League's Buffalo office. "It would seem," quipped Lambert, "that the disreputable League for Americanism is trying to get into good company; but the President of the Medical Society of the County of Erie, has fallen into bad company."[72] The treasurer of the county society, Albert T. Lytle, was not at all pleased with his president's ties to the insurance interests and surreptitiously arranged with Lambert to mail out 3,000 copies of a pamphlet exposing the League, on condition that his identity would not be revealed. "If I am to be of any use in the future at this end of the State I will have carefully to avoid any activity along any lines even remotely associated with health insurance," he explained.[73]

By mid-1920 even the AALL, discouraged by recent setbacks and the reactionary temper of the times, was noticeably losing interest in compulsory health insurance.[74] In 1921 Socialist Assemblyman Samuel Orr of the Bronx introduced a health insurance bill, but, as Rooney happily reported, "this bill has slept very quietly in Committee."[75] Now that victory was theirs, the opponents of insurance could afford to be smug. They had not only defeated the reformers, but had succeeded at the same time in welding the medical profession into an effective and articulate political force. "Gentlemen, this Health Insurance agitation has been good for us," said Henry Lyle Winter to a group of Rochester physicians as the debate drew to a close. "If it goes no farther it will have brought us more firmly together than any other thing which has ever come to us."[76]

9. DEATH BY HYSTERIA

I think that my profession will get over its present state of hysteria just as my ancestors got over the Salem witchcraft. They had it bad at that time, and the profession has "got it bad" now.

Dr. Alexander Lambert, President of the AMA, January 1920

Health Insurance, as such, is a dead issue in the United States.

Report of the Committee on Medical Economics,
Medical Society of the State of New York, May 1925

The postwar debate over compulsory health insurance, as we have seen in New York, often degenerated into polemics and name-calling. Paradoxically, as the prospects for passage declined, stridency increased; and as physicians won more and more concessions, they grew increasingly less inclined to compromise.[1] Although no state came as close as New York to enacting health insurance legislation, the subject attracted considerable attention elsewhere, particularly in the Midwest, where the medical societies of Illinois, Indiana, and Michigan banded together to combat it.[2]

The center of Midwestern opposition was Chicago, Illinois, the home of Edward H. Ochsner. In August 1919 Ochsner's friend, Charles J. Whalen, assumed the editorship of the *Illinois Medical Journal,* the most widely circulated of the state medical magazines, and quickly emerged as the shrillest critic of health insurance west of O'Reilly. As he himself put it, he "left no stone unturned, even at the expense of some personal and business friendships, to clean up the evil conditions that menace medicine . . . and lower the social status of the profession."[3] In editorials bristling with invective, he damned the proponents of health insurance—Bolsheviks, anarchists, Russians with Americanized names, and unpatriotic alien physicians who should be deported[4]—while at the same time lauding the work of Hoffman, O'Reilly, and the National Civic Federation and praising Ochsner as being "the greatest authority in the world on medical economics."[5]

The health insurance committees of the Chicago Medical Society and the Illinois State Medical Society, on both of which sat Whalen and Ochsner, were equally unrestrained in condemning social insurance, which they saw as a fraud perpetrated by "parlor bolsheviks and publicity seekers." Because the committees had earlier fallen into the Bolshevik "trap" of believing that compulsory health insurance was inevitable, and consequently had offered constructive suggestions, they were now hurt and angry.[6] Early in 1921 Ochsner, as chairman of the Chicago group, invited O'Reilly, "the Patrick Henry of the American medical profession," to address a mass meeting of Chicago doctors, dentists, and druggists, an event that only further inflamed the anti-insurance passions of Midwestern physicians.[7]

In Indiana, where physicians only belatedly became interested in compulsory health insurance, the state medical society took a strong position against the "menace,"[8] and at times the editor of the state medical journal seemed to be competing with Whalen for the honor of publishing the most spirited denunciations of socialized medicine and its supporters. In Michigan it was much the same story. Late into the fray, Michigan doctors made up for lost time by importing Ochsner and other Illinois critics of health insurance to address their annual meeting in 1920, where they apparently voted to join the anti-insurance forces.[9] The local opposition leader was "a real live wire" named George E. Frothingham, who, as chairman of the state society's Committee on Civic and Industrial Relations, concluded that the only people who wanted compulsory health insurance were plutocrats, professors, professional uplifters, and "parlor Bolsheviks."[10] Even Wisconsin physicians, previously the most enthusiastic for health insurance, succumbed to postwar disillusionment, and in 1919 the chairman of the Committee on Social Insurance of the state medical society recommended—with apparent relief—that his committee be discharged, now that the threat of insurance had passed.[11]

A reaction against compulsory health insurance was also evident in the Northeast. The Pennsylvania State Medical Society, the only state society besides Wisconsin to have endorsed health insurance, reversed itself in 1920 and resolved:

That the Medical Society of the State of Pennsylvania, while deeply interested in all measures that will aid in solving the problem of providing proper care and treatment for the sick and injured, especially among the working classes, in the light of our present knowledge, places itself on record as opposed to the enactment of a statute providing for Compulsory Health Insurance, believing that it would not only fail of accomplishing the desired end, but would also impose a heavy and unnecessary financial burden upon the people of this commonwealth, and would lower the present high and efficient standards of medical service.[12]

That same year the Connecticut State Medical Society passed a mildly worded resolution stating that compulsory health insurance was not needed in the state and "that its establishment would be harmful to the Society, to the practice of medicine, and to the people and State of Connecticut." The state's physicians did not, however, feel strongly on the issue. Only 30 percent bothered to reply to a questionnaire on health insurance, and of these "not more than a dozen took sides for or against compulsory health insurance."[13] By 1921 the state medical societies of Delaware, New Hampshire, and New Jersey had also declared against compulsory health insurance.[14]

Outside the industrial states of the Northeast and Midwest few physicians participated in the health insurance debate. By 1919 the issue had already been settled in California, and it never became a major topic of discussion in primarily agricultural states. In the South racial considerations made passage of insurance legislation, with open panels and free choice of physician, even less likely. As W. S. Rankin, secretary of the North Carolina State Board of Health, explained, the health insurance movement would probably be delayed in coming to North Carolina and other Southern states for two reasons:

First, when compulsory social insurance comes up in the South it will immediately become entangled with the race problem; the explanation is obvious. Second, when the matter is proposed for serious consideration in North Carolina, we will have to deal with the fact that compulsory social insurance has never been applied to a class of the self-employed, to an agricultural population. It is a measure designed for the wage-earning group, and so far in practice it has been limited almost entirely to the wage-earning group. As we all know, North Carolina is about 90 per cent agricultural.[15]

The reports of the state health insurance commissions also show opinion turning against health insurance legislation after the war. Of the four commissions reporting before 1919, three—Massachusetts (1917), California (1917), and New Jersey (1918)—favored it, while only one—Massachusetts (1918)—opposed it. In 1919 the score was even. The Ohio, New York, and second California commissions were positive; Connecticut, Illinois, and Wisconsin were negative; Pennsylvania was undecided.[16]

Despite the many differences between the AALL's model bill and the insurance systems of Germany and Great Britain,[17] most of the commissions wrestled with the question of whether the European experiments had succeeded or failed. And like everyone else, they found much of the evidence contradictory.[18] The most frequently cited source on the negative side was Frederick Hoffman, who used the press of the Prudential Life Insurance

Company to turn out a continuous stream of pamphlets exposing not only foreign health insurance but its "unpatriotic" American advocates as well. Generally he argued that health insurance abroad had been "disastrous," debasing the medical profession and duping the workers. During the summer and fall of 1919 he traveled to England "to ascertain the facts" first hand and returned home to say that medical attendance had deteriorated "to the point of mediocrity." Physicians were spending most of their time dealing with "imaginary and often only trivial compaints," and medical diagnosis had become "routine and casual." Only one conclusion could be drawn, he said: "that national health insurance is a conspicuous failure both as regards the interests of the public and the interests of the medical profession."[19]

Although some commissions accepted Hoffman's pronouncements as authoritative and *JAMA* declared them worthy of "serious consideration,"[20] others questioned both his objectivity and his methodology. English physicians complained that "he didn't even know the terms of the Act," "that he could only see one side of the question," and that he had made invalid comparisons. "He goes to see the very worst of the physicians practising in the poorest quarters of the city," said the secretary of the London Panel Committee, "and then compares their work with that of the highest-paid men in London, and considers that he's made a decent comparison between the men under the Act and the men outside it."[21] The *British Medical Journal,* in reviewing one of his pamphlets, deplored his "odious" tone and noted that while he had been "industrious in collecting opinions and facts," his "opinions appear to have been all of one colour, and his facts are in some instances incomplete and in some others misinterpreted."[22]

Hoffman's views of the German system appeared equally suspect, especially when it was pointed out that his own earlier testimony contradicted what he was now saying. In 1910, shortly after returning from a visit to Germany, he had told a Massachusetts commission that German social insurance had "been of vast benefit to the people and to the nation at large." But just nine years later he attributed this embarrassing lapse to his former limited opportunities for observation and to the possibility that he had temporarily come "under the influence of the German mind and German thought."[23]

Considerable evidence suggests that Hoffman's hatred of compulsory health insurance colored his view of its operation in Europe, particularly in Great Britain. A mail survey of British physicians conducted in late 1919 and early 1920 by the New York Academy of Medicine reveals significant differences of opinion, particularly between those working under the Act and those not. Of the ten extant replies, four give a favorable picture of the Health Insurance Act, three offer no opinion or are neutral, and three oppose it. One of these, written by a Harley Street practitioner who apparently had never served on a panel, reported that "the better class of general practitioners greatly dislike the whole thing!" Another London physician claimed that the Act had set back the progress of medicine "by about fifty years." But, according to one Hyde Park specialist, such comments were of little value. Consultants like himself, he wrote, talked a lot about health insurance but were generally ignorant on the subject. The replies from panel physicians outside the metropolis bear him out. A Sheffield doctor with a large panel practice, for example, described the Act as "good for both doctor and patient" and said that at a recent medical meeting in his town not a single man had voted for a resolution against health insurance, introduced by a visiting physician.[24]

Several Americans visited England in 1919 and 1920 to judge health insurance for themselves. In the summer of 1919 John Andrews arranged to spend six weeks in England gathering data on the operation of the Act. While there he interviewed officials at the Ministry of Health, the staff of the British Medical Association, labor leaders, and physicians, all of whom left him with the conviction that compulsory health insurance was unquestionably a success. Its administration was "unnecessarily cumbersome" and its benefits were inadequate, but on the whole it seemed to be "working more smoothly than it deserves!"[25] Several of his British contacts later sent him written evaluations of the National Insurance Act, and not one opposed it.[26] Typical was the attitude of Alfred Cox, secretary of the British Medical Association, who wrote that "the present system, with all its shortcomings, is a distinct advance" over what existed before.[27]

A year later three more American visitors confirmed Andrews' findings. Joseph P. Chamberlain, who had helped to draft the model bill, reported that his visit had "entirely dissipated" the impression given by Hoffman that health insurance was a failure overseas.[28] Similarly, William T. Ramsey and Ordway Tead, representing the Pennsylvania Health Insurance Commission, spent a month in England and returned convinced that both patients and physicians were benefitting under the Act. It was simply not true, they said, that panel service "involves an ignominious, subordinate and undignified relationship of the doctor to the rest of the community. Nothing can be further from the truth if the British experience can be taken as proof."[29]

But Hoffman's negative image persisted despite these positive testimonies. Thus in May 1921 Lambert and Andrews arranged with the editors of *JAMA* to have Cox give the British Medical Association's position on national health insurance. The British act, even with its limited coverage and other imperfections, has improved both the public health and the private wealth of physicians, wrote the BMA secretary in a three-part article. "I can confidently say that not one doctor in 1,000 who is doing National Health work would willingly go back to the old system."[30] His words, however, fell on deaf ears. *JAMA*'s London Correspondent continued his exposés of British health insurance, and *JAMA*'s editors persisted in denying that National Insurance had bettered the health of the English working classes.[31]

The radically different views of the European experience were a source of puzzlement to many. How, they asked, was it possible for two parties to observe the same evidence and yet see such dissimilar things? Hoffman not surprisingly attributed any favorable account of German health insurance to "the insidiousness of the German propaganda,"[32] but this explanation, even if true, hardly explains the English case. The editor of the *New York State Journal of Medicine* suggested that the diversity of opinions stemmed largely from "the source of the information" upon which conclusions were based.[33] But Hoffman and Andrews, for example, often talked with the same persons and presumably heard the same things.[34] Allowing for some perversity and the common tendency to see what one wants to see, I suspect that much of the confusion resulted from a misunderstanding of the British willingness to air complaints. "In all their criticism [the British] assume the fundamental worth, the continuance and the improvement of the act," explained one perceptive visitor. "And only as the investigator realizes their assumptions, will his construction of the facts keep him on the right track."[35]

During the final phase of the American debate over compulsory health insurance the anti-insurance physicians of New York and Illinois orchestrated an attempt to have the AMA officially declare its opposition to government health insurance and all other forms of "state medicine." Early in 1919, following the conclusion of the war, the AMA reorganized its Social Insurance Committee, inactive since May 1917. The only survivor from the original committee was Alexander Lambert, who resumed his duties as chairman. Joining him were Frederick Van Sickle, president of the Medical Society of the State of Pennsylvania and author of its 1916 resolution endorsing health insurance; and Malcolm L. Harris, a Chicago surgeon and chairman of the AMA's Judicial Council, who was still undecided about health insurance.[36] Conspicuously absent was I. M. Rubinow, who was off in Jerusalem having "a fairly interesting time teaching the principles of socialized medicine to the people of Asia," but obviously disappointed to be missing out on events back home.[37] In announcing the reconstitution of the committee, the Council on Health and Public Instruction lamented the "unqualified and often unreasoning opposition" of the majority of physicians at a time when "the most careful, painstaking patient and disinterested study" was so badly needed.[38]

The need for additional study was also a topic of discussion at the February 1919 meeting of the AMA Board of Trustees, who apparently paid little attention to the subject earlier. At this meeting Lambert submitted a report on the current status of the insurance movement, noting in particular the opposition of Hoffman, Ochsner, and the Insurance Economics Society of America. In his opinion, the state most likely to enact health insurance legislation was Ohio, largely because of Emery R. Hayhurst's recent studies of industrial health hazards in that state. Lambert also reminded the trustees of the AMA's position on the subject, namely that any law must provide adequate medical representation on administrative bodies, payment in proportion to work done, free choice of physician, and the separation of medical supervision from the professional care of the sick. The trustees took no action, although at least one of them, Wendell C. Phillips, seemed eager to vote against compulsory health insurance.[39]

The first of several attempts to get the House of Delegates officially to oppose health insurance took place at the AMA's 1919 annual session, held in Atlantic City in early June. Eden V. Delphey had been agitating for an anti-insurance resolution for over a year,[40] and just prior to the Atlantic City convention the state medical societies of both New York and Illinois instructed their delegates "to introduce a resolution against compulsory health insurance in the House of Delegates of the American Medical Association, and to support it in every way possible."[41] Their efforts failed, however. In an early vote the House of Delegates unanimously commended Lambert's Committee on Social Insurance for "refraining to make any definite recommendations on the subject at this time," and the Reference Committee felt that a New York-sponsored resolution against health insurance was both premature and an unwarranted reversal of the earlier action. Thus the resolution was tabled.[42]

The foes of compulsory health insurance lost this initial battle, but their movement continued to gain momentum. In January 1920 Lambert, who had refrained from even mentioning social insurance in his Atlantic City presidential address,[43] complained about the irrational behavior of his colleagues. "I think my profession will get over its present state of hysteria just as my ancestors got over the Salem witchcraft," he wrote a discouraged

John Andrews. "They had it bad at that time, and the profession has 'got it bad' now."[44] Symptomatic of this condition were the protests being sent to the AMA trustees regarding the activities of Lambert and his Committee on Social Insurance, particularly the pamphlets prepared by Rubinow. In response to these complaints, the executive committee of the Board of Trustees on January 2 ordered that no more of these tracts be sent out. Furthermore, they blamed Lambert personally for having ever allowed them to be printed.[45] Shortly afterward one of his own committee members, the previously neutral Harris, joined the opposition and began publicly denouncing compulsory health insurance.[46]

As the next session of the AMA approached, critics of health insurance, stung by their setback the previous year, began making preparations to insure against a second defeat. Once again Delphey contacted medical societies throughout the nation, urging them to elect only delegates pledged to oppose compulsory health insurance at the April meeting in New Orleans.[47] And once more the state societies of New York and Illinois endorsed his anti-insurance resolution.[48] Joining them this time was the Michigan State Medical Society, whose *Journal* was advocating that Lambert and other proponents of insurance be "sat on" in New Orleans.[49]

The Louisiana session got off to an inauspicious start, from a pro-insurance point of view, when for only the second time since 1916 (the other being in 1918 during the war) the Committee on Social Insurance made no report. Instead, the Council on Health and Public Instruction notified the delegates that the committee's work had ended because the defeat of the Davenport bill made further legislative action highly unlikely. Now somewhat embarrassed for having created the committee in the first place, the Council lamely explained that its only objective—obviously accomplished—had been "to arouse the medical profession to a discussion of this subject and to prevent the premature adoption of any such measures in this country as in England without the full knowledge of the medical profession."[50] Frederick R. Green, the Council's secretary and the person most repsonsible for the existence of the Committee on Social Insurance, was by this time describing compulsory health insurance as an "economically, socially and scientifically unsound" proposition supported only by "radicals."[51]

When the speaker of the House of Delegates opened the floor for new business on the first day of the session, a representative from New York introduced a resolution—supported by James F. Rooney of New York, Charles J. Whalen of Illinois, and F. C. Warnshuis of Michigan—placing the AMA on record as opposing all forms of compulsory health insurance.[52] At

Lambert's suggestion the resolution was referred to the Reference Committee on Hygiene and Public Health, whose chairman, J. W. Schereschewsky of the U.S. Public Health Service, supported compulsory health insurance. According to one account, Lambert then showed up uninvited at the meeting of the Reference Committee, where together with the chairman he tried to railroad the group into reporting against the New York resolution without even discussing it. A majority, however, insisted on allowing representatives from New York, Illinois, and Michigan to argue their case, and the committee subsequently voted four to one to recommend approval of the anti-insurance resolution.[53] Schereschewsky, the lone dissenter, reluctantly agreed to make the vote unanimous. The resolution, as amended by the committee, read:

> *Resolved,* That the American Medical Association declares its opposition to the institution of any plan embodying the system of compulsory contributory insurance against illness, or any other plan of compulsory insurance which provides for medical service to be rendered contributors or their dependents, provided, controlled, or regulated by any state or the Federal Government.[54]

When the resolution finally reached the floor of the House on April 27, Lambert made one last desperate attempt to sway opinion against the measure; but the presiding officer ruled him out of order, and the delegates voted overwhelmingly for the resolution.[55]

"Ninety per cent. of the delegates were in favor of this resolution," wrote the defeated doctor to John Andrews. "I could not do anything with them."

> I am becoming more and more convinced that the quickest way to bring the doctors into a more reasonable point of view is to go ahead without any regard to them, continue the provisions that you have in your present last bill, which is a perfectly fair proposition to them and hammer the situation from the inadequacy of present medical care and refusal of physicians to improve the situation socially. That will throw them on the defensive. You are on the defensive now, and their position is stronger than yours.

In the future he recommended cutting loose from "the traditions of Rubinow and the German basis" and offering a broadly based plan not restricted to certain social classes.[56]

In victory, Lambert's critics were anything but gracious. "'They hung Haman on the scaffold he had prepared for Mordecai,'" crowed Whalen in the *Illinois Medical Journal,* "and the same poetic justice was meted out to Dr. Lambert at New Orleans when he was hung on one of the many scaffolds of destruction he so energetically prepared for the execution of the medical profession of the United States."[57] To humiliate their former nemesis even more, the Illinois and Indiana state medical journals took to ridiculing Lambert, a pioneer in the treatment of drug addiction and alcoholism, for his "drug and booze cure" and for his naiveté in thinking that alcoholism could be treated medically. The House of Delegates of the Illinois State Medical Society went so far as to pass a resolution, aimed at embarrassing Lambert, asking *JAMA* to discontinue advertising the Towns Sanitarium, with which the New York physician was connected.[58]

Not everyone, however, applauded the action at New Orleans. "This resolution is decidedly a negative way to solve the problems which have been pushed to the front with the agitation for health insurance," commented the progressive *Modern Medicine*. "It will help very little in constructive leadership on these problems."[59] In some circles the rejection of health insurance further tarnished the medical profession's already stained public image. As the social worker Edward T. Devine pointed out, it was hard to reconcile the profession's unabashedly economic criticisms of health insurance with its claim not to be working "for filthy lucre, but for the satisfaction of preserving life and safeguarding health." Did the doctors really think, he asked rhetorically, "that the obstructive, dog-in-the-manger, pettifogging tactics by which health insurance is now opposed in their name will add to the esteem in which the medical profession is held?"[60]

The landslide victory in November of Republican presidential candidate Warren G. Harding, a declared foe of compulsory health insurance, over James M. Cox of Ohio, a Democratic advocate of the measure, symbolized the nation's rejection of reform and drove the supporters of health insurance to despair.[61] A "tide of reaction" is sweeping the country, observed Andrews in a letter to AALL members following the national election.[62] But Lambert somehow remained optimistic in spite of it all. "Don't feel so badly over the apparent collapse of moral endeavor to better things," he wrote his young associate. "Every action has its contrary and equal reaction and all improvements run in waves like fever charts. . . . This is not a tide of reaction, it is only a relaxation of effort."[63]

Time would eventually prove Lambert to be right, but not for over a decade. In the meantime the reaction against social insurance increased rather than diminished. The defenders of laissez-faire medicine, emboldened by their success in turning back the menace of compulsory health insurance, now turned their attention to other related evils that threatened to result "in the socialization of medicine, the enslavement of the medical profession and the pauperization of the public." Before health insurance "went into coma or expired," reported the Committee on Health Insurance of the Illinois State Medical Society, "the beast gave birth to a litter answering to the name of State or County Subsidized Health Centers, Rural hospitals under University control, State Medicine, and the Sheppard-Towner Bill."[64]

The Sheppard-Towner bill, passed by Congress in 1921 at the insistence of the newly enfranchised women of America, presented the most immediate threat. To assist in reducing the inexcusably high infant mortality rate among the poor, it provided federal funds to the states for such activities as establishing prenatal care centers, conducting child health conferences, supporting visiting nurse programs, and distributing informational literature.[65] Following the defeat of its health insurance bill the AALL threw "its modest resources" into the campaign for passage of the Sheppard-Towner proposal,[66] which only fed suspicions that the bill was simply an "entering wedge" for compulsory health insurance. "This bill," wrote the splenetic editor of the *Illinois Medical Journal,* "is a menace and represents another piece of destructive legislation sponsored by endocrine perverts, derailed meno-pausics and a lot of other men and women who have been bitten by that fatal parasite, the upliftus putrifaciens . . . all of whom are working overtime to devise means to destroy the country."[67]

Faced with the imminent passage of this bill, as well as numerous proposals for government-subsidized health centers and diagnostic clinics, the crusaders against health insurance laid plans to extend the AMA's condemnation of insurance to cover all phases of "state medicine," a term seldom defined precisely but commonly used to designate anything that seemed to infringe on the private practice of medicine.[68] Prior to the AMA's 1921 annual session in Boston the medical societies of New York, Illinois, and Michigan requested their respective delegations to introduce a resolution declaring their emphatic opposition "to 'State Medicine,' and to any schemes for 'Health Centers,' 'Group Medicine,' 'Diagnostic Clinics,' 'Compulsory Health Insurance,' either wholly or partly controlled, operated or subsidized by the State or National Government."[69] In Boston the delegates from New Hampshire joined Delphey of New York, Whalen of Illinois, and J. D. Brook of Michigan in supporting such a resolution. However, the Reference Committee on Legislation and Public Relations, to which it was referred, refused to approve it. Instead, it offered a positively worded substitute: "Resolved, By the House of Delegates of the American Medical Association that it approves and endorses all proper activities and policies of state and federal governments directed to the prevention of disease and the preservation of the public health." In a close vote, allegedly decided by the delegates from the scientific sections, the substitute motion won approval.[70]

Unfortunately, the Boston session ended on a sour note that tended to drown out this progressive declaration. When Frank Billings, a former president of the AMA and one of its most distinguished members, came up for re-election to the Board of Trustees, some physicians, apparently led by Ochsner, tried to discredit him by distributing a circular quoting him as saying in 1916 that he was "unequivocally in favor of compulsory insurance and the protection of maternity." Only after the harassed old man publicly recanted his earlier statement, saying that he had long since concluded that "health insurance was not applicable to the United States," did the House of Delegates reaffirm its confidence in him. The acrimonious debate left the few remaining defenders of compulsory health insurance with the distinct impression that their ideological opponents would like nothing better than to try them for treason and boil them in oil.[71]

Frustrated by their failure in Boston, the foes of state medicine immediately began preparing for a "show down" in St. Louis the following year.[72] Many simply desired the passage of a resolution against state medicine, but a few, like O'Reilly of Brooklyn, demanded a thorough housecleaning of the AMA, including stripping the delegates from scientific sections of their right to vote.[73] The O'Reillys lost, but the House of Delegates did in 1922 approve the following resolution introduced by James F. Rooney:

> The American Medical Association hereby declares its opposition to all forms of "state medicine," because of the ultimate harm that would come thereby to the public weal through such form of medical practice.
> "State medicine" is hereby defined for the purpose of this resolution to be any form of medical treatment, provided, conducted, controlled or subsidized by the federal or any state government, or municipality, excepting such service as is provided by the Army, Navy or Public Health Service, and that which is necessary for the control of communicable diseases, the treatment of mental disease, the treatment of the indigent sick, and such other services as may be approved by and administered under the direction of or by a local county medical society, and are not disapproved by the state medical society of which it is a component part.[74]

The passage of this resolution against any further encroachments by the government into the private practice of medicine effectively ended organized medicine's brief flirtation with reform. Following the St. Louis meeting the subject of compulsory health insurance disappeared as quickly as it had appeared in the years before World War I. There was no more talk of "inevitability," and even the AALL by the end of 1922 had given up lobbying for new social legislation and was now content merely to hold "the ground already gained."[75] "Health Insurance, as such, is a dead issue in the United States," reported the Committee on Medical Economics of the New York State Medical Society in 1925. "It is not conceivable that any serious effort will again be made to subsidize medicine as the hand-maiden of the public."[76] The victorious New York physicians had every reason to be confident, but they failed to reckon with economic disaster. Within a few years the Great Depression would once again force the nation to consider the possible merits of compulsory health insurance.[77]

EPILOGUE

Between 1916 and 1920 the attitude of American physicians toward compulsory health insurance changed dramatically. Following a brief flirtation, the medical profession abruptly turned its back on what came to be called "socialized medicine." Not surprisingly, this about-face has prompted considerable comment.

A decade ago John Gordon Freymann argued that the AMA's rejection of reform resulted from "an abdication of responsibility by the scientific and academic leaders of American medicine." He identified several factors that seemed to have led these physicians to relinquish their position of leadership: in the wake of the Flexner report medical education had become a self-sufficient and independent enterprise, full-time clinical positions had freed many academics from the struggle for economic survival, and the growth of specialization had turned the attention of medical scientists from state and national medical societies to specialty societies.[1]

The available evidence, however, does not support this argument. The composition of the AMA's House of Delegates did indeed change between 1916 and 1920, but the new delegates were neither less academic nor less scientific than their predecessors. In fact, between 1917 and 1920 the percentage of academics among state delegates *increased* from 15.4 to 18.3, while nonspecialists and small-town physicians lost representation.[2] (See Table 1) Furthermore, throughout the early 1920s the presidency of the AMA remained in the hands of an academic-scientific elite, some of whom pointedly rejected the reactionary ways of their colleagues. Among Alexander Lambert's immediate successors to the office were William C. Braisted, Surgeon General of the United States Navy; Hubert Work, one of the nation's best-known psychiatrists; George E. deSchweinitz, an outstanding ophthalmologist; and Ray Lyman Wilbur, the distinguished president of Stanford University. In his 1923 presidential address Wilbur took the profession to task for its "hit and miss individualistic methods" of practicing medicine and sternly warned the conservatives that they could not prevent reforms merely by "calling them bolshevik or socialistic or pro-German." We can guide future progress, he admonished them, "if we get away from the brake and begin to steer."[3]

110

Table 1. Composition of the AMA House of Delegates

	Population of Residence			
	Over 100,000	25,000-100,000	10,000-25,000	Under 10,000
1917	38.5%	23.1%	15.4%	23.1%
1920	45.9%	21.1%	16.5%	16.5%

	Type of Practice	
	Specialist-Academic	Nonspecialist
1917	44.9%	55.1%
1920	56.9%	43.1%

Sources: *JAMA,* 1917, *68:* 1354; 1920, *74:* 839-40; AMA, *American Medical Directory* (1918, 1921). The *JAMA* list of state delegates for 1917 is about 60 percent complete; for 1920, about 84 percent. These figures do not include the fourteen section delegates or the two delegates from Puerto Rico and the Philippines.

The foes of compulsory health insurance certainly were not aware of any abdication. As late as 1921 they were directing their sharpest barbs at Lambert and the delegates from the scientific sections who opposed their resolutions against state medicine. If the scientific and academic leaders did lose interest in the AMA, they did so *after* the conservative shift and perhaps as a result of it.

According to another school of thought, most recently represented by Elton Rayack, Carleton B. Chapman, and John M. Talmadge, the "conservative revolution" within the medical profession resulted not from a failure of leadership but from a rank-and-file takeover by those who feared "that the fee-for-service principle would be eliminated and medical incomes lowered, that the free choice of physician would disappear, and that the patient-doctor relationship would be destroyed." These practitioners, Rayack maintains, simply drowned out the handful of progressive physicians "in a virtual flood of opposition."[4] As Chapman and Talmadge describe it, the Eden Delpheys of the profession, the grass-roots general practitioners, overthrew their traditional leaders, like Lambert and Billings, "whose education had gone beyond the minimal requirements for the M.D. degree, who had moved from general to specialty practice, and who were prominent in academic medicine and research." The result was "a sharp and permanent swing to the right within organized medicine."[5]

This explanation, though partially accurate, suffers from oversimplification. Opponents of compulsory health insurance did fear loss of income, regimentation, and destruction of the traditional doctor-patient relationship; but their opposition continued even after fee-for-service and free choice were guaranteed, and the majority of rank-and-file physicians remained surprisingly apathetic throughout the debate. Moreover, this view creates a false dichotomy between specialists and nonspecialists. Early support for health insurance was not confined to a small well-educated elite, any more than opposition was restricted to general practitioners. Ochsner, an archcritic of compulsory health insurance, was a prominent Chicago surgeon, and the fiery O'Reilly was an expert in legal medicine.

But most important of all, the theory of a grass-roots takeover ignores the large number of physicians who switched sides during the debate. The doctors who rejected compulsory health insurance in 1920 were by and large the same ones who had welcomed—or at least tolerated—it only four years earlier. The best example of this is the AMA's Frederick Green, but others, like Billings and M. L. Harris, experienced similar conversions.[6] In 1916 even Delphey, Whalen, and Webster—later intransigent opponents of insurance—were willing, if not eager, to accept it.[7]

Entire medical organizations reacted in the same way. The Pennsylvania State Medical Society, which formally endorsed compulsory health insurance in 1916, rescinded its action after the war, and the sponsor of the pro-insurance resolution, Van Sickle, withdrew his support.[8] The physicians of Wisconsin undoubtedly would have followed suit, but by 1919 the threat of insurance legislation had disappeared in that state.[9] And by 1920 the once-sympathetic homeopaths had changed their minds about health insurance.[10]

No single cause adequately explains these changes. World War I and its aftermath clearly poisoned the atmosphere of debate, but medical opposition to compulsory health insurance antedated America's entry into the conflict.[11] Opportunism seems to explain the behavior of Green and some of his associates in the AMA who, according to Rubinow, rapidly adjusted their views to bring them into conformity with "what appeared to be the profession's attitude."[12] But this still leaves the question of why the profession's attitude changed—a question that can only be answered by examining the experience of physicians between 1916 and 1920.

During this period nothing seems to have played a greater role in molding opinion than money. In the early days of the debate, when poorly paid American physicians believed that they, like their British brethren, might benefit financially from compulsory health insurance, it seemed like an attractive idea. However, as the debate progressed and reports began circulating that the British medical profession was suffering under health insurance, the prospect of financial gain appeared less certain. At the same time the incomes of physicians were increasing without insurance. The average income of taxed physicians in Wisconsin, for example, rose 41 percent between 1916 and 1919.[13] Wartime inflation was responsible for much of this, but an unprecedented decline in the total number of physicians undoubtedly had some effect.[14]

Another important factor was the medical profession's discovery that compulsory health insurance was not inevitable, as it had formerly thought. Before 1917 there seemed to be no escape from social insurance. It had already swept through Western Europe, and reform-conscious Americans were certain that it would soon leap the Atlantic. Realistic physicians simply resigned themselves to making the best of it. But as Progressivism waned and legislators balked at passing more reform bills, doctors began to realize that they had a choice. And why, many reasoned, should they take a chance on the unknown if it was not absolutely necessary? With each legislative setback, talk of inevitability grew fainter and fainter, until by 1920 not even Andrews and Lambert seriously believed it.

Finally, many American physicians had their first encounter with social insurance between 1916 and 1920, and though they seldom mentioned it during the debate over compulsory health insurance, their experience undoubtedly colored their attitudes.[15] Beginning in 1911 most states passed laws making employers legally responsible for on-the-job injuries, but few of these early workmen's compensation acts provided comprehensive medical benefits. During the war, however, most states added such provisions or liberalized existing ones, giving American doctors their first taste of social insurance. For many it was not pleasant. Employers often took out accident insurance with commercial companies, which then either contracted with physicians to care for the injured or paid local practitioners according to an arbitrary fee schedule.[16] Neither arrangement pleased the medical profession, which accused the insurance carriers of paying below-normal fees and of providing inadequate medical care. "Pus and politics go together," warned one AMA publication on workmen's compensation. "A stingy man hires a poor surgeon and begets many infections and much disability."[17] This was scarcely a recommendation for compulsory health insurance.

Although compulsory health insurance ceased to attract much attention after 1920, its influence on the medical profession was noticeable for years to come. Having finally turned it away from the front door, frightened physicians remained nervously on guard lest it "sneak in through the side door"[18] — in the guise, perhaps, of health centers, government-subsidized prenatal care, or even voluntary health insurance, which in the early 1930s was seen as "the forerunner of compulsory insurance."[19] When compulsory health insurance did reappear, during the Depression, doctors successfully fought it off in part with arguments they had developed and tested two decades earlier. Thus it seems, as Michael Davis suggested years ago, that the practical result of the campaign for compulsory health insurance between 1912 and 1920 was "to stimulate opposition more than to widen support."[20]

A NOTE ON SOURCES

During the past half-century a considerable body of literature on the campaign for compulsory health insurance has accumulated. Most accounts, however, are of little value, and even the best tend to overlook events below the national level. An exception is Arthur J. Viseltear's excellent "Compulsory Health Insurance in California, 1915-18," *Journal of the History of Medicine and Allied Sciences*, 1969, *24:* 151-82.

Among the most useful of the early surveys are John R. Commons and A. J. Altmeyer's "The Health Insurance Movement in the United States," which appeared in the report of the Ohio Health and Old Age Insurance Commission, *Health, Health Insurance, Old Age Pensions: Report, Recommendations, Dissenting Opinions* (Columbus, 1919), pp. 287-311; and Pierce Williams' discussion in *The Purchase of Medical Care through Fixed Periodic Payment* (New York: National Bureau of Economic Research, 1932), pp. 34-57. Also of interest are the retrospective analyses by participants in the debate; see, for example, Isaac M. Rubinow, *The Quest for Security* (New York: Henry Holt, 1934), and Michael M. Davis, *Medical Care for Tomorrow* (New York: Harper and Brothers, 1955).

The best recent study is Roy Lubove's chapter "Made in Germany" in *The Struggle for Social Security, 1900-1935* (Cambridge: Harvard University Press, 1969), pp. 66-90. Also worth consulting are Odin W. Anderson, "Health Insurance in the United States, 1910-1920," *Journal of the History of Medicine and Allied Sciences*, 1950, *5:* 363-96, subsequently incorporated into *The Uneasy Equilibrium: Private and Public Financing of Health Services in the United States, 1875-1965* (New Haven, Conn.: College & University Press, 1968); Forrest A. Walker, "Compulsory Health Insurance: 'The Next Great Step in Social Legislation,'" *Journal of American History*, 1969, *56:* 290-304; and Hace Sorel Tishler, *Self-Reliance and Social Security, 1870-1917* (Port Washington, N.Y.: Kennikat Press, 1971), which emphasizes the role of the National Civic Federation in preventing the passage of health insurance legislation.

Most accounts of the AMA's role in the debate suffer from either superficial analysis or inadequate documentation. Morris Fishbein's *History of the American Medical Association, 1847 to 1947* (Philadelphia: W. B. Saunders, 1947) has the advantage of using the minutes of the AMA Board of Trustees, but unfortunately it offers little more than year-by-year summaries of activities. Nevertheless, it is considerably more reliable than the garbled account that appears in his *Autobiography* (New York: Doubleday, 1969), pp. 185-89. Other discussions of the AMA and compulsory health insurance can be found in James G. Burrow, *AMA: Voice of American Medicine* (Baltimore: Johns Hopkins Press, 1963), pp. 132-51; John Gordon Freymann, "Leadership in American Medicine: A Matter of Personal Responsibility," *New England Journal of Medicine*, 1964,

115

270: 710-20; Elton Rayack, *Professional Power and American Medicine: The Economics of the American Medical Association* (Cleveland: World Publishing Co., 1967), pp. 136-46; and Carleton B. Chapman and John M. Talmadge. "The Evolution of the Right to Health Concept in the United States," *Pharos,* 1971, *34:* 30-51, which appeared in an abridged version as "Historical and Political Background of Federal Health Care Legislation," *Law and Contemporary Problems,* 1970, *35:* 334-47.

Lloyd Pierce's dissertation on "The Activities of the American Association for Labor Legislation in Behalf of Social Security and Protective Labor Legislation" (University of Wisconsin, 1953) remains the most useful history of the AALL, although a fresh interpretation is badly needed. Of less value is T. Charles McKinney's largely derivitive study of "The Role of Organized Labor in the Quest for Compulsory Health Insurance, 1912-1965" (Ph.D. dissertation, University of Wisconsin, 1969).

Some of the best sources for the history of American medicine in the early twentieth century are the reports of the various state commissions on social insurance. The most comprehensive are: Ohio Health and Old Age Insurance Commission, *Health, Health Insurance, Old Age Pensions: Report, Recommendations, Dissenting Opinions* (Columbus, 1919); *Report of the Health Insurance Commission of Pennsylvania* (Harrisburg, 1919); and *Report of the Health Insurance Commission of the State of Illinois* (Springfield, 1919). But see also the New Jersey Commission on Old Age, Insurance, and Pensions, *Report on Health Insurance* (Rahway, 1917); *Report of the Social Insurance Commission of the State of California* (Sacramento, 1917); and the Wisconsin *Report of the Special Committee on Social Insurance* (Madison, 1919).

Periodicals

Much of the material upon which this study is based was discovered by means of an issue-by-issue search of the following publications:

Albany Medical Annals
American Journal of Nursing
American Journal of Public Health
American Labor Legislation Review
American Medical Association Bulletin
American Medicine
Boston Medical and Surgical Journal
British Medical Journal
Buffalo Medical Journal
Bulletin of the American College of Surgeons
Bulletin of the Insurance Economics Society of America
Bulletin of the Medical and Chirurgical Faculty of the State of Maryland
California State Journal of Medicine
Canadian Medical Association Journal
Colorado Medicine
Dental Cosmos

Eclectic Medical Journal
Illinois Medical Journal
Indiana State Medical Association Journal
Journal of Sociologic Medicine
Journal of the American Medical Association
Journal of the American Pharmaceutical Association
Journal of the Missouri State Medical Association
Journal of the National Dental Association
Journal of the South Carolina Medical Association
Lancet
Long Island Medical Journal
Maryland Medical Journal
Medical Record
Midland Druggist and Pharmaceutical Review
Minnesota Medicine
Mississippi Valley Medical Journal
Modern Hospital
Modern Medicine
New Orleans Medical and Surgical Journal
New York Medical Journal
New York State Journal of Medicine
New York Times
Pennsylvania Medical Journal
Proceedings of the Connecticut State Medical Society
Rhode Island Medical Journal
Southern Medical Journal
Survey
Transactions of the Medical Society of the State of North Carolina
Transactions of the Mississippi State Medical Association
Transactions of the New Hampshire Medical Society
Wisconsin Medical Journal

Index Medicus proved to be helpful in locating articles on compulsory health insurance in other state and regional publications, as well as in such out-of-the-way journals as *Medical Insurance and Health Conservation* and the *Railway Surgical Journal.*

Manuscripts

By far the most important collection of unpublished documents relating to compulsory health insurance is among the papers of the American Association for Labor Legislation in the Labor-Management Documentation Center, M. P. Catherwood Library, Cornell University (now available on microfilm from the Microfilming Corporation of America, Glen Rock, New Jersey). The Labor-Management Documentation Center also has a transcript of the public hearings of the Social Insurance Commission of the State of California, held in San Francisco, Nov. 20-22, 1916, and the papers of Isaac M. Rubinow. Unfortunately, Rubinow's personal files do not begin until 1929.

The Department of Manuscripts and University Archives, Cornell University Libraries, has assembled one of the most extensive collections of county-medical-society records in the country. Especially valuable for my study were the minute books of the Chautauqua County Medical Society, the Dutchess County Medical Club, the Medical Society of the County of Monroe, the Onondaga County Medical Society, and the Tompkins County Medical Society. The records of the Medical Society of the County of Kings, in the possession of the Academy of Medicine of Brooklyn, also contain numerous references to compulsory health insurance.

Another excellent collection of county society records is in the State Historical Society of Wisconsin, but the Wisconsin documents say virtually nothing about compulsory health insurance in the years between 1912 and 1920. The same is true of the minutes of the Milwaukee Medical Society, held by the Milwaukee Academy of Medicine.

In the Archives of the American Medical Association in Chicago are the minutes of the Board of Trustees and the Council on Health and Public Instruction. The records of the former, however, are not generally open for public inspection, nor may they be quoted when made available. The minutes of the Judicial Council, still in the Council's possession, could not be found for the period before 1922, although I have reason to believe they are extant.

The Medical Society of the State of New York and the Massachusetts Medical Society both have extensive minutes from 1912 to 1920, but these reports are also available in the *New York State Journal of Medicine* and the *Boston Medical and Surgical Journal.*

The papers of the Public Health Committee of the New York Academy of Medicine include a number of letters from British physicians describing life under the Health Insurance Act, plus E. H. Lewinski-Corwin's 1915 report on health insurance. The Michael M. Davis Collection in the Academy Library contains little of interest for the years before 1920, but the Library does have two (individually cataloged) Eden V. Delphey letters urging opposition to compulsory health insurance.

My greatest disappointment was learning that the bulk of Alexander Lambert's papers had been destroyed only weeks before I finally tracked down their custodian. The surviving documents, still in private hands, are primarily reprints of articles on tuberculosis and correspondence relating to the Roosevelt Memorial Association, of which Lambert was an officer.

NOTES

CHAPTER 1

1. *Historical Statistics of the United States, 1789-1945* (Washington: Government Printing Office, 1949), pp. 25-26, 65, 67, 231; Arthur S. Link, *American Epoch: A History of the United States since the 1890's,* 2d ed. (New York: Alfred A. Knopf, 1963), pp. 19-23.

2. Richard Harrison Shryock, *The Development of Modern Medicine* (New York: Hafner Publishing Co., 1969), p. 318.

3. Frederick L. Hoffman, "American Mortality Progress during the Last Half Century," in *A Half Century of Public Health,* ed. Mazyck P. Ravenal (New York: American Public Health Association, 1912), pp. 99-101.

4. Ohio Health and Old Age Insurance Commission, *Health, Health Insurance, Old Age Pensions: Report, Recommendations, Dissenting Opinions* (Columbus, 1919), pp. 44-45.

5. Lee K. Frankel and Louis I. Dublin, "Community Sickness Survey: Rochester, N.Y., September, 1915," *U.S. Public Health Reports,* 1916, *31:* 423-35.

6. Ibid., pp. 435-37.

7. B. S. Warren and Edgar Sydenstricker, *Health Insurance: Its Relation to Public Health,* Public Health Bull. No. 76 (Washington: Government Printing Office, 1916), p. 6.

8. Frankel and Dublin, "Community Sickness Survey," p. 634.

9. *Report of the Health Insurance Commission of Pennsylvania* (Harrisburg: J. L. L. Kuhn, 1919), pp. 32, 96-97. The Pennsylvania Commission estimated that "the average cost of medical care for every employee's family is between $30.00 and $50.00 a year"; ibid., p. 32. An Ohio study of 508 families showed "an average cost of $41.79 for medical care and $8.59 for dental care"; Ohio Health and Old Age Insurance Commission, *Health,* p. 115.

10. *Report of the Health Insurance Commission of Pennsylvania,* p. 108.

11. Ibid., pp. 98-99, 143.

12. Abraham Flexner, *Medical Education in the United States and Canada* (New York: Carnegie Foundation for the Advancement of Teaching, 1910), p. 14. In 1910 there were 135,000 physicians in America, and over 4,000 new graduates joining the ranks every year; *Historical Statistics of the U.S.,* p. 50.

13. Committee on Social Insurance, *Statistics Regarding the Medical Profession,* Social Insurance Series Pamphlet No. 7 (Chicago: AMA, [1917]), pp. 66, 68. On the alleged physician shortage, see also Henry Lyle Winter, "A Side Light on Health Insurance," *New York State J. Med.,* 1918, *18:* 199.

14. Committee on Social Insurance, *Statistics,* pp. 11, 19-20.

15. On the impact of the automobile on American medical care, see the Report of the Committee on Medical Economics, Med. Soc. State of New York, *New York State J. Med.,* 1921, *21:* 203; and Michael L. Berger, "The Influence of the Automobile on Rural Health Care, 1900-1929," *J. Hist. Med.,* 1973, *28:* 319-35.

16. Committee on Social Insurance, *Statistics,* pp. 28-31. This study also showed that the American medical profession was composed primarily of native born white males. In 1910 only 2 percent of American physicians were black, and only 6 percent were women.

17. George Thomas Palmer, "Health Insurance from the Standpoint of the Physician," *Illinois Med. J.,* 1917, *31:* 6. Dr. Palmer was president of the Illinois State Association for the Prevention of Tuberculosis and of the Illinois Public Health and Welfare Association.

18. *Report of the Health Insurance Commission of the State of Illinois* (Springfield: Illinois State Journal, 1919), p. 80.

19. J. M. Toner, "Statistics of Regular Medical Associations and Hospitals of the United States," AMA, *Trans.*, 1873, *24:* 314; *Historical Statistics of the U.S.*, p. 51.

20. Morris J. Vogel, "Boston's Hospitals, 1870-1930: A Social History" (Ph.D. diss., Univ. of Chicago, 1974), pp. 1-2.

21. *Report of the Health Insurance Commission of the State of Illinois*, p. 85.

22. Charles E. Rosenberg, "Social Class and Medical Care in Nineteenth-Century America: The Rise and Fall of the Dispensary," *J. Hist. Med.*, 1974, *29:* 32-54; *Report of the Health Insurance Commission of the State of Illinois*, pp. 90-93.

23. Health insurance commissions in Illinois, Pennsylvania, and California all agreed that no more than a third of wage-earners in their states had voluntary health insurance. See ibid., p. 146; *Report of the Health Insurance Commission of Pennsylvania*, p. 34; and *Report of the Social Insurance Commission of the State of California* (Sacramento: California State Printing Office, 1917), p. 88.

24. *Report of the Health Insurance Commission of Pennsylvania*, p. 34; Ohio Health and Old Age Insurance Commission, *Health*, p. 121. On early health insurance plans in America, see Edgar Sydenstricker, "Existing Agencies for Health Insurance in the United States," *Proc. Conf. Social Insurance*, Dec. 5-9, 1916, Bull. U.S. Bureau of Labor Statistics No. 212 (Washington: Government Printing Office, 1917), pp. 430-75; and Jerome L. Schwartz, "Early History of Prepaid Medical Care Plans," *Bull. Hist. Med.*, 1965, *39:* 450-75.

25. *Report of the Social Insurance Commission of the State of California*, pp. 81-82; *Report of the Health Insurance Commission of Pennsylvania*, p. 34; Ohio Health and Old Age Insurance Commission, *Health*, p. 120.

26. *Report of the Social Insurance Commission of the State of California*, p. 84.

27. *Report of the Health Insurance Commission of Pennsylvania*, p. 149. See also *Report of the Social Insurance Commission of the State of California*, pp. 87-88. In addition to life insurance companies offering coverage against sickness, there were commercial hospital associations that provided medical and hospital insurance for a limited number of diseases; ibid., pp. 85-87.

28. I. M. Rubinow, *Social Insurance: With Special Reference to American Conditions* (New York: Henry Holt, 1913), p. 297.

29. *Report of the Social Insurance Commission of the State of California*, pp. 102-4; "Sickness Insurance," *Charities and the Commons*, 1908, *21:* 473.

30. Charles H. Lemon, "Discussion," *Wisconsin Med. J.*, 1918, *17:* 230-31.

31. *Report of the Health Insurance Commission of Pennsylvania*, p. 34.

32. For accounts of governmental health activities, see Bernhard J. Stern, *Medical Services by Government: Local, State, and Federal* (New York: Commonwealth Fund, 1946); and Milton I. Roemer, "Government's Role in American Medicine—A Brief Historical Survey," *Bull. Hist. Med.*, 1945, *18:* 146-68.

33. Milton Terris, "An Early System of Compulsory Health Insurance in the United States, 1798-1884," ibid., 1944, *15:* 433-44. See also Robert Strauss, *Medical Care for Seamen: The Origin of Public Medical Service in the United States* (New Haven: Yale University Press, 1950); and Harry J. Campbell, "The Congressional Debate over the Seaman's Sickness and Disability Act of 1798: The Origins of the Continuing Debate on the Socialization of American Medicine," *Bull. Hist. Med.*, 1974, *48:* 523-26.

34. Roemer, "Government's Role in American Medicine," pp. 158-60.

35. Ibid., pp. 148-49; Stern, *Medical Services by Government*, pp. 90-95; Myles Standish, "The Socialization of the Practice of Medicine," *Boston Med. & Surg. J.*, 1918, *178:* 838.

36. Robert T. Legge, "Students' Health Insurance at the University of California," *Calif. State J. Med.*, 1917, *15:* 102-4; Edith Shatto King, "Health Insurance in a Student

Community," *Survey*, 1916, *36:* 619-20. Beginning in 1911 many states also enacted workmen's compensation laws, which, though they seldom covered industrial diseases, did provide for surgical care in case of accident. See Roy Lubove, *The Struggle for Social Security, 1900-1935* (Cambridge: Harvard University Press, 1968), pp. 45-65.

37. James H. Cassedy, *Charles V. Chapin and the Public Health Movement* (Cambridge: Harvard University Press, 1962), p. 176.

38. Stern, *Medical Services by Government*, pp. 6-12; Roemer, "Government's Role in American Medicine," p. 147.

39. *Report of the Social Insurance Commission of the State of California*, p. 43.

40. *Report of the Health Insurance Commission of the State of Illinois*, p. 93.

41. Report of Committee on Dispensary Abuse, Med. Soc. County of New York, 1912, *New York State J. Med.*, 1913, *13:* 48-53. I am indebted to Dr. Gert Brieger for bringing this report to my attention.

42. "Medical Economics," ibid., 1915, *15:* 290.

43. John Duffy, *A History of Public Health in New York City, 1866-1966* (New York: Russell Sage Foundation, 1974), pp. 238-76; George Rosen, "The First Neighborhood Health Center Movement—Its Rise and Fall." *Am. J. Public Health.*, 1971, *61:* 1628-29.

44. Duffy, *A History of Public Health in New York City*, pp. 269-70.

45. "Sickness Insurance," *Boston Med. & Surg. J.*, 1916, *174:* 248; Frederick L. Van Sickle, "Social Insurance against Accidents (Workman's Compensation Laws)," *J. Sociologic Med.*, 1916, *17:* 292.

46. Report of the Judicial Council, *JAMA*, 1913, *60:* 1998.

47. "Medical Economics," *New York State J. Med.*, 1915, *15:* 289.

48. Report of the Judicial Council, p. 1996. For one explanation of the physicians' plight, see Moses Scholtz, "Compulsory State Health Insurance and the Medical Profession," *Lancet-Clinic*, 1916, *115:* 400-401.

49. Committee on Social Insurance, *Statistics*, p. 81.

50. Ibid., pp. 81, 87. According to Flexner in 1910, full professors in the nation's 100 financially strongest institutions averaged $2,500 annually, while instructors teaching in their first ten years averaged $1,325. This proved to him "that a large financial inducement is not indispensable, provided a man is doing what he likes." Flexner, *Medical Education*, pp. 44-45.

51. Committee on Social Insurance, *Statistics*, p. 88.

52. See, e.g., the Report of the Judicial Council, p. 1996; and Van Sickle, "Social Insurance against Accidents," p. 292.

53. Michael M. Davis, "Existing Conditions of Medical Practice, Forms of Service under Health Insurance, and Preventive Work," *Proc. Conf. Social Insurance*, pp. 676-77. See also Rosemary Stevens, *American Medicine and the Public Interest* (New Haven: Yale University Press, 1971), p. 134.

54. Ohio Health and Old Age Insurance Commission, *Health*, p. 132; *Report of the Health Insurance Commission of the State of Illinois*, p. 79.

55. Ibid., p. 81.

56. Ohio Health and Old Age Insurance Commission, *Health*, pp. 131-32. See also "Socializing Medicine," *Minnesota Med.*, 1920, *3:* 85.

57. For a summary of the European experience, see Shryock, *Development of Modern Medicine*, pp. 381-402. Elsewhere, Shryock noted that the need for compulsory health insurance arose partly from the adoption of higher licensing standards, which decreased the number of second-class German "doctors" and drove up the cost of medical services. Shryock, *Medical Licensing in America, 1650-1965* (Baltimore: Johns Hopkins Press, 1967), p. 12.

58. I. M. Rubinow, *Standards of Health Insurance* (New York: Henry Holt and Co., 1916), p. 20.

59. Rubinow, *Social Insurance*, p. 26.
60. William Harbutt Dawson, *Social Insurance in Germany, 1883-1911* (New York: Charles Scribner's Sons, n.d.), p. 11. The following account is based on Dawson and Rubinow, *Standards of Health Insurance*.
61. This account of British compulsory health insurance is based on Bentley B. Gilbert, *The Evolution of National Insurance in Great Britain: The Origins of the Welfare State* (London: Michael Joseph, 1966); Rubinow, *Standards of Health Insurance;* Report of the Committee on Social Insurance, *JAMA,* 1916, *66:* 1951-85; and Jeanne L. Brand, *Doctors and the State: The British Medical Profession and Government Action in Public Health, 1870-1912* (Baltimore: Johns Hopkins Press, 1965), pp. 209-31.
62. On the friendly societies, see P. H. J. H. Gosden, *The Friendly Societies in England, 1815-1875* (Manchester: University of Manchester Press, 1961).
63. Rubinow, *Standards of Health Insurance*, p. 195.

CHAPTER 2

1. On Progressivism, see, e.g., Arthur A. Ekirch, Jr., *Progressivism in America: A Study of the Era from Theodore Roosevelt to Woodrow Wilson* (New York: New Viewpoints, 1974); and Robert H. Wiebe, *The Search for Order, 1877-1920* (New York: Hill and Wang, 1967).
2. Sidney Fine, *Laissez Faire and the General-Welfare State: A Study of Conflict in American Thought, 1865-1901* (Ann Arbor: University of Michigan Press, 1956), pp. 353-78.
3. William J. Kerby, *Proc. Conf. on Social Insurance,* Dec. 5-9, 1916, Bull. U.S. Bureau of Labor Statistics No. 212 (Washington: Government Printing Office, 1917), p. 419; Roy Lubove, *The Struggle for Social Security, 1900-1935* (Cambridge: Harvard University Press, 1968), pp. 2-3.
4. John R. Commons and A. J. Altmeyer, "The Health Insurance Movement in the United States," in Ohio Health and Old Age Insurance Commission, *Health, Health Insurance, Old Age Pensions: Report, Recommendations, Dissenting Opinions* (Columbus, 1919), pp. 287-311. Although an avowed Socialist, I. M. Rubinow claimed to have prepared the plank on social insurance for the Progressive Party; Rubinow to George Derby, Jan. 18, 1926, Rubinow Papers, Cornell University.
5. Irwin Yellowitz, *Labor and the Progressive Movement in New York State, 1897-1916* (Ithaca, N.Y.: Cornell University Press, 1965), p. 55.
6. Lloyd F. Pierce, "The Activities of the American Association for Labor Legislation in Behalf of Social Security and Protective Labor Legislation" (Ph.D. diss., Univ. of Wisconsin, 1953), pp. 1-21.
7. Ibid., pp. 62-79.
8. John B. Andrews, *Amer. Labor Legislation Rev.* [hereafter cited as *ALLR*], 1916, *6:* 121.
9. W. F. Willoughby to J. B. Andrews, Jan 31, 1913; J. B. Andrews to Miles Dawson, Feb. 10, 1913, AALL Papers, Cornell University.
10. F. L. Hoffman to J. B. Andrews, Feb. 11, 1913, AALL Papers.
11. F. L. Hoffman to Irving Fisher, Feb. 5, 1917, AALL Papers.
12. I. M. Rubinow, *Social Insurance, with Special Reference to American Conditions* (New York: Henry Holt, 1913), p. iii. For biographical data, see I. M. Rubinow to George Derby, Jan. 18, 1926; and Neva R. Deardorff, "Isaac Max Rubinow," *Dictionary of American Biography,* supplement II, pp. 585-87. Rubinow's membership in the Socialist Party is mentioned in a letter to John Martin, July 1, 1913, AALL Papers.

13. I. M. Rubinow, "First American Conference on Social Insurance," *Survey*, 1913, *30:* 478-80.

14. "Against Compulsory Health Insurance," *Penn. Med. J.*, 1918, *22:* 164.

15. Victor C. Vaughan, "Medical Ideals," *Wisconsin Med. J.*, 1915, *13:* 297.

16. James H. Cassedy, "Frederick Ludwig Hoffman," *Dictionary of American Biography*, supplement IV, pp. 384-85; Hoffman to Fisher, Feb. 5, 1917.

17. The following discussion, except where otherwise noted, is based on the committee's "Brief for Health Insurance," *ALLR*, 1916, *6:* 155-236.

18. Robert H. Bremner, *From the Depths: The Discovery of Poverty in the United States* (New York: New York University Press, 1956), pp. xi, 131, 138.

19. John B. Andrews, "Outline of Work, 1913," *ALLR*, 1914, *4:* 150; J. B. Andrews, "Outline of Work, 1914," ibid., 1915, *5:* 153-54.

20. Committee on Social Insurance, "Preliminary Standards for Sickness Insurance," ibid., 1914, *4:* 595-96; "Memorandum Re:—Necessary Standards of Sickness Insurance," *ca.* June, 1914, AALL Papers.

21. J. P. Chamberlain to J. B. Andrews, June 22 and July 15, 1914; F. L. Hoffman to J. B. Andrews, July 7 and Oct. 21, 1914, AALL Papers.

22. Arthur Mann, "British Thought and American Reformers of the Progressive Era," *Mississippi Valley Hist. Rev.*, 1956, *42:* 672.

23. J. P. Chamberlain to J. B. Andrews, Jan. 7, 1914, AALL Papers; J. P. Chamberlain, "The Practicability of Compulsory Sickness Insurance in America," *ALLR*, 1914, *4:* 50.

24. J. P. Chamberlain to J. B. Andrews, June 11, 1914; Katharine Coman to J. B. Andrews, July 21, 1914, AALL Papers; Olga S. Halsey, "Compulsory Health Insurance in Great Britain," *ALLR*, 1916, *6:* 127-37.

25. J. P. Chamberlain to J. B. Andrews, Dec. 11, 1914, AALL Papers; "Unemployment and Compensation in a Pennsylvania Setting," *Survey*, 1915, *33:* 403.

26. F. L. Hoffman to J. B. Andrews, Jan. 13, 1915, AALL Papers.

27. F. L. Hoffman to J. B. Andrews, July 7, 1914, AALL Papers; F. L. Hoffman, "Discussion," *JAMA*, 1915, *65:* 2060; F. L. Hoffman, *American Problems in Social Insurance* (pamphlet reprint from *Proc.*, 41st Annual Meeting of the National Conference of Charities and Correction, 1914), pp. 7-9.

28. J. P. Chamberlain to J. B. Andrews, June 10, 1915; F. L. Hoffman to Irving Fisher, Feb. 5, 1917, AALL Papers. Henderson, for unknown reasons, also seems to have left the committee by the time a tentative draft appeared.

29. Pierce, "Activities of the AALL," p. 258.

30. K. Coman to J. B. Andrews, Aug. 4, 1914, AALL Papers.

31. J. B. Andrews to K. Coman, Aug. 7, 1914, AALL Papers.

32. William S. Gottheil to J. B. Andrews, Feb. 25, 1916, AALL Papers.

33. Morris Fishbein, *A History of the American Medical Association, 1847 to 1947* (Philadelphia: W. B. Saunders, 1947), pp. 744-47. Lambert is credited with having convinced Roosevelt to back William C. Gorgas against Theodore P. Shonts in the controversy over mosquito control in Panama, and thus indirectly of having saved the canal project; see Hermann Hagedorn, *The Roosevelt Family of Sagamore Hill* (New York: Macmillan, 1954), pp. 240-42.

34. John Duffy, "Sigismund Schulz Goldwater," *Dictionary of American Biography*, supplement III, pp. 312-13; "A Biographical Note," in S. S. Goldwater, *On Hospitals* (New York: Macmillan, 1947), pp. xix-xl.

35. Robert H. Bremner, "Lillian D. Wald," *Notable American Women, 1607-1950*, ed. Edward T. James (Cambridge: Harvard University Press, 1971), III, 526-29.

36. John B. Andrews, "Secretary's Report, 1915," *ALLR*, 1916, *6:* 104; *Health Insurance: Standards and Tentative Draft of an Act* (New York: AALL, 1916), p. 7. See also

I. M. Rubinow, *Standards of Health Insurance* (New York: Henry Holt, 1916), pp. iii-iv.
37. John B. Andrews, "Health Insurance and the Prevention of Tuberculosis," *Medical Record,* 1916, *89:* 370. The following description of the tentative draft is based on Henry R. Seager, "Plan for a Health Insurance Act," *ALLR,* 1916, *6:* 21-25; and *Health Insurance: Standards and Tentative Draft of an Act,* which, except for the addition of sections relating to medical care, is virtually identical to the first tentative draft.
38. J. B. Andrews, "Secretary's Report, 1915," *ALLR,* 1916, *6:* 105.
39. Minutes of the Council on Health and Public Instruction, Dec. 11, 1915, AMA Archives; F. R. Green to J. B. Andrews, Nov. 11, 1915, AALL Papers.

CHAPTER 3

1. Minutes of the House of Delegates, June 21, 1915, *JAMA,* 1915, *65:* 64; *Historical Statistics of the United States, 1789-1945* (Washington: Government Printing Office, 1949), p. 50. Fewer than a third of American physicians were dues-paying fellows of the AMA.
2. James G. Burrow, *AMA: Voice of American Medicine* (Baltimore: Johns Hopkins Press, 1963), pp. 16-26.
3. Ibid., pp. 14-16; Morris Fishbein, *A History of the American Medical Association, 1847 to 1947* (Philadelphia: W. B. Saunders, 1947), pp. 32-34. In 1882 the AMA voted to accept persons applying for membership.
4. Burrow, *AMA,* p. 19.
5. Ibid., pp. 27-29; Fishbein, *History of the AMA,* pp. 204-13.
6. On the traditional conservatism of the AMA, see Richard Harrison Shryock, *Medical Licensing in America, 1650-1965* (Baltimore: Johns Hopkins Press, 1967), p. 94.
7. Burrow, *AMA,* pp. 67-139. See also Manfred Waserman, "The Quest for a National Health Department in the Progressive Era," *Bull. Hist. Med.,* 1975, *49:* 353-80.
8. Thomas Neville Bonner estimates that "no less than fifteen thousand American medical men . . . undertook some kind of serious study in a German university between 1870 and 1914"; *American Doctors and German Universities: A Chapter in International Intellectual Relations, 1870-1914* (Lincoln: University of Nebraska Press, 1963), p. 23.
9. "Sick Insurance and Sanatoria in Germany," *JAMA,* 1899, *32:* 1459.
10. "National Insurance in Germany," ibid., 1910, *54:* 225-26.
11. Vienna Correspondent, "Proposed Insurance of Wage-Earners," ibid., 1910, *52:* 396.
12. "Organization of the Profession in Germany," ibid., 1903, *40:* 1229.
13. Berlin Correspondent, "Debate on Social Insurance Bill," ibid., 1910, *55:* 515-16. See also his communications, ibid., 1910, *54:* 62, 1221, 1704. The identity of the Berlin Correspondent at this time is uncertain; in 1913, when Morris Fishbein joined *JAMA* as an assistant to the editor, the Berlin contact was the influential editor of the *Deutsche Medizinische Wochenschrift,* Julius Schwalbe. Morris Fishbein to R.L.N., May 28, 1974.
14. Ibid.
15. "The Relation of the Physician to Compulsory Sickness and Invalidity Insurance," *JAMA,* 1906, *46:* 1471. Other physicians at this meeting echoed Billings' view; see ibid., pp. 1470-72. See also "Workingmen's Insurance in Germany," ibid., 1907, *48:* 1448.
16. "National Insurance in Germany," ibid., 1910, *54:* 225-26. It is difficult, if not impossible, to assign specific authorship to *JAMA* editorials. During the early decades of this century *JAMA* published editorials by about forty different guest editors, each identified by a secret number known only to Simmons and Fishbein. Most of the editorials underwent heavy editing, and thus often turned into group projects. Interview with Dr. Morris Fishbein, May 16, 1974.

17. "Club Practice and State Insurance in Great Britain, Germany, Austria and France," *JAMA*, 1910, *54:* 725-26.

18. Prior to World War I *JAMA*'s London Correspondent was the editor of a small British medical magazine. Fishbein interview, May 16, 1974.

19. "Socializing the British Medical Profession," *JAMA*, 1912, *59:* 1890. The *Medical Record* reached a similar conclusion; see "State Sickness and Invalidity Insurance," *Medical Record,* 1911, *79:* 344.

20. "Socializing the British Medical Profession," p. 1890. See also the comments on this editorial in *Survey,* 1912, *29:* 373-74.

21. "Socializing the British Medical Profession," pp. 1890-91.

22. Algernon T. Bristow, "The Doctor's Future in Relation to National Medical Insurance," *JAMA*, 1913, *60:* 153; "Social Insurance and the 'Doctor's Future,'" *Survey,* 1912, *29:* 318.

23. "Socializing the British Medical Profession," p. 1891. On the inevitability of compulsory health insurance in America, see also J. N. Davis, "Health Insurance," *JAMA*, 1912, *58:* 681; and Arthur C. Jacobson, "Socialization of the Profession," *Long Island Medical Journal,* 1912, *6:* 404-5. Davis welcomed the prospect; Jacobson feared it.

24. "State Medicine in Great Britain," *New York State Med. J.,* 1912, *12:* 689. See also "Sacrificing Self for the General Good," *JAMA*, 1912, *59:* 2075. Norway, where almost all physicians were members of the medical association and had no trouble securing their demands, provided an even better example of the benefits of a united profession; see "Medical Insurance Abroad," ibid., 1913, *61:* 2316.

25. "Socializing the British Medical Profession," p. 1891.

26. For typical dispatches from the London Correspondent on the working of the National Insurance Act, see *JAMA*, 1913, *60:* 531, 607-8, 1472.

27. London Correspondent, "The National Insurance Act and the Scarcity of Physicians," ibid., 1914, *62:* 218.

28. London Correspondent, "Mr. Lloyd-George on the Insurance Act," ibid., p. 789; and "Medical Remuneration under the Insurance Act," ibid., p. 945. In 1914 the secretary of the British Medical Association told a visiting South Carolina physician that the incomes of general practitioners had, "in many instances, quadrupled"; *J. South Carolina Med. Assn.,* 1916, *12:* 260.

29. London Correspondent, "The National Insurance Act," *JAMA*, 1913, *61:* 289.

30. London Correspondent, "The National Insurance Act," ibid., p. 2254; Report of the Judicial Council, ibid., 1915, *65:* 85.

31. London Correspondent, "Sickness Benefit Claims under the Insurance Act," ibid., 1915, *64:* 1863.

32. "Benefits of the British Insurance Act," ibid., 1913, *61:* 296; "Proprietary Prescribing in Great Britain," ibid., p. 872.

33. According to F. R. Green, the question of compulsory health insurance was "both an ethical and an economic one"; Minutes of the Council on Health and Public Instruction, Dec. 11, 1915, AMA Archives.

34. W. F. Zierath, "The Socialization of Medicine," *Wisconsin Med. J.,* 1915, *13:* 306.

35. Robert A. Allen, "State Insurance against Sickness," *JAMA*, 1914, *63:* 187.

36. "Social Insurance in California," ibid., 1915, *65:* 1560.

37. James P. Warbasse, "The Socialization of Medicine," ibid., 1914, *63:* 266. For other examples of early admiration of the British plan, see William Francis Campbell, "Economic Factors in the Doctor's Future," *Long Island Med. J.,* 1913, *7:* 138-41; Ranulph Hudston, "The National Insurance Act of Great Britain: A Review," *Colorado Med.,* 1913, *10:* 292-98; and B. S. Warren, "Sickness Insurance: A Preventive of Charity Practice," *JAMA,* 1915, *65:* 2056-59. In 1915 E. H. Lewinski-Corwin, executive secretary of the Public Health Committee of the New York Academy of Medicine, presented a report recommending compulsory health insurance on the basis of the European experience; "Notes and

Suggestions Concerning Health Insurance," Nov. 18, 1915, Records of the Public Health Committee, New York Academy of Medicine.

38. Fishbein interview, May 16, 1974.

39. Report of the Judicial Council, *JAMA,* 1915, *65:* 73-92.

40. "Frederick Robin Green," ibid., 1929, *92:* 1539. According to Dr. Morris Fishbein, it is likely that "most (if not all)" of the early *JAMA* editorials on health insurance were initially prepared by Green, then edited by Simmons, and finally polished for publication by Fishbein; Fishbein to R.L.N., May 28, 1974.

41. Lloyd F. Pierce, "The Activities of the American Association for Labor Legislation in Behalf of Social Security and Protective Labor Legislation" (Ph.D. diss., Univ. of Wisconsin, 1953); Minutes of the Council on Health and Public Instruction, Nov. 1, 1913, AMA Archives; F. R. Green to J. B. Andrews, Jan. 15, 1913, AALL Papers.

42. J. B. Andrews to F. R. Green, Aug. 11, 1914, AALL Papers.

43. Andrews' letter is mentioned in the minutes of the Council on Health and Public Instruction, Dec. 11, 1915, AMA Archives.

44. F. R. Green to J. B. Andrews, Nov. 11, 1915, AALL Papers.

45. Ibid.

46. Ibid.

47. "A Model Bill for Health Insurance," *JAMA,* 1915, *65:* 1824.

48. Minutes of the Council on Health and Public Instruction, Dec. 11, 1915. Favill died before the end of winter.

49. "Cooperation in Industrial Health Insurance Legislation," *JAMA,* 1915, *65:* 2247.

50. "Report of the Committee on Social Insurance," ibid., 1916, *66:* 1951. This report, signed by Lambert, gives the erroneous impression that Favill first suggested an AMA committee on social insurance, that he did so in Jan., 1916, and that he, not Lambert, appointed Cotton to the committee.

51. Ibid.; Minutes of the Council on Health and Public Instruction, Oct. 28, 1916, AMA Archives.

52. Ibid. The date of Rubinow's joining the AMA is given in I. M. Rubinow to George Derby, Jan. 18, 1926, Rubinow Papers.

CHAPTER 4

1. J. B. Andrews to John R. Commons, March 16, 1916, AALL Papers; *Proc. Conf. Social Insurance,* Dec. 5-9, 1916, Bull. U.S. Bureau of Labor Statistics No. 212 (Washington: Government Printing Office, 1917), pp. 608, 618. Ironically, its capitulation to Kelley cost the AALL some feminist support; see Pauline Newman, "What Will Health Insurance Mean to the Insured?" *Am. J. Nursing,* 1917, *17:* 945, 951.

2. Eden V. Delphey to Olga Halsey, Feb. 2, 1916, AALL Papers. Halsey assured Delphey that the AALL was "not trying to starve the medical profession"; Halsey to Delphey, Feb. 5, 1916, ibid.

3. Eden V. Delphey, Letter to the Editor, *JAMA,* 1917, *68:* 1500; ibid., 1925, *85:* 1657. Edward H. Ochsner credited Delphey with being the "first man to see the danger" of compulsory health insurance; Ochsner, "Compulsory State Health Insurance," *Railway Surgical J.,* 1920, *27:* 77.

4. *Proc. Conf. Social Insurance,* pp. 717-19.

5. H. G. W[ebster], "Health Insurance," *Long Island Med. J.,* 1916, *10:* 123-25; and "The Mills Bill," ibid., pp. 159-60.

6. "Opposition to the Health Insurance Bill," *Medical Record,* 1916, *89:* 423-24.

7. "Health Insurance," *Buffalo Med. J.,* 1916, *71:* 419; "The Problem of the Independent Poor," ibid., pp. 522-23.

8. "Health Insurance," *Albany Medical Annals,* 1916, *37:* 141.

9. "The Mills Health Insurance Act," *New York Med. J.,* 1916, *103:* 557. See also "Insurance against Sickness," ibid., p. 173.

10. William S. Gottheil to J. B. Andrews, Feb. 25, 1916, AALL Papers. In this letter Gottheil said that he would support the Mills bill if "certain changes" were made.

11. Samuel J. Kopetzky, "Comment on the Mills Bill, Senate 236," *New York State J. Med.,* 1916, *16:* 157-58.

12. "Oppose Health Insurance," *New York Times,* Feb. 29, 1916, p. 9.

13. "Compulsory Health Insurance," ibid., March 8, 1917, p. 10.

14. "Opposition to the Health Insurance Bill," pp. 423-24.

15. "Health Insurance," *American Med.,* 1916, *22:* 140-42.

16. Olga Halsey, "Hearing on Health Insurance Bill (Senate No. 236), Albany, March 14, 1916," AALL Papers; J. B. Andrews to John R. Commons, March 16, 1916, ibid.; "Health Insurance Plan under Fire," *New York Times,* March 15, 1916, p. 4. Andrews told Commons that Pauline Newman of the International Ladies' Garment Workers' Union had urgently requested "that maternity benefits be restored to the bill."

17. J. P. Chamberlain to J. B. Andrews, March 15, 1916, AALL Papers.

18. James F. Rooney, Report of the Committee on Legislation, *New York State J. Med.,* 1916, *16:* 309-10.

19. J. B. Andrews to AALL Members, May 1, 1916, AALL Papers.

20. Chamberlain to Andrews, March 15, 1916.

21. "Study Health Insurance," *New York Times,* April 18, 1916, p. 22; *New York Senate J.,* 1916, *1:* 708; *New York Assembly J.,* 1916, *3:* 2169. On a copy of the bill in the AALL Papers J. B. Andrews penciled "Ogden L. Mills. Handed to him at his home in N.Y.C. Mch. 20 for introduction."

22. "The Next Step in Health Insurance," *New York Med. J.,* 1916, *103:* 798; "Health Insurance," ibid., 1916, *104:* 317. During the latter part of the year the *New York Med. J.* carried a series of articles on "Health Insurance from the Viewpoint of the Physician"; see, e.g., ibid., pp. 301-4 (A. C. Burnham); pp. 1050-53 (Ira S. Wile); and pp. 1191-93 (Eden V. Delphey).

23. H. G. W[ebster], "Preparedness," *Long Island Med. J.,* 1916, *10:* 244-45.

24. Minutes of the Council, March 15, 1916, *New York State J. Med.,* 1916, *16:* 217; Frank Van Fleet, Letter to the Editor, *Medical Record,* 1916, *89:* 480.

25. Minutes of the House of Delegates, May 15, 1916, *New York State J. Med.,* 1916, *16:* 323; S. F. Kopetzky to the Social Insurance Commission of the State of California, Oct. 5, 1916, *Report of the Social Insurance Commission of the State of California* (Sacramento: California State Printing Office, 1917), pp. 278-79; "Meeting of the Committee on Medical Economics," *New York State J. Med.,* 1916, *16:* 605-6.

26. J. P. Chamberlain to Olga Halsey, April 3, 1916, AALL Papers.

27. *Health Insurance: Standards and Tentative Draft of an Act,* 3d ed. (New York: AALL, 1916), pp. 14-15. The bill also allowed for a system of salaried physicians, or a combination of salaried physicians and panel physicians, where local conditions warranted it.

28. Ibid., pp. 15, 28-32.

29. Ibid., pp. 11-12.

30. "Meeting of the Committee on Medical Economics," *New York State J. Med.,* 1916, *16:* 605-6.

31. Ibid., p. 612; Eden V. Delphey, "Compulsory Health Insurance from the Point of View of the General Practitioner," ibid., pp. 601-4.

32. Minutes of the Council, Dec. 9, 1916, ibid., 1917, *17:* 47-48.

33. Olga S. Halsey, "Hearing on Health Insurance Bill (Senate No. 236), Albany, March 14, 1916," AALL Papers; J. B. Andrews to Samuel McCune Lindsay, Feb. 2, 1916, ibid.

34. "Health Insurance Now a Practical Issue," *Survey,* 1916, *35:* 691.

35. F. J. Cotton, "A Consideration of Workingmen's Accident and Sickness Insurance in Their Relation to the Medical Profession," *Boston Med. & Surg. J.,* 1916, 175: 893-94.

36. Annual Meeting of the Council, June 6, 1916, ibid., 1916, *174:* 921-22.

37. Stated Meeting of the Council, Oct. 4, 1916, ibid., 1916, *175:* 584-85.

38. "Aim to Insure the Sick," *New York Times,* June 9, 1916, p. 5. Immediately after the bill to create a commission passed the legislature, J. B. Andrews asked C. W. Doten to suggest to the governor that Doten, Cotton, Felix Frankfurter, and Michael Davis, who seems to be "taking the keenest interest in the subject," be appointed to the commission; Andrews to Doten, June 3, 1916, AALL Papers. On Davis's early reform activities, see Ralph E. Pumphrey, "Michael M. Davis and the Development of the Health Care Movement, 1900-1928," *Societas,* 1972, *2:* 27-41.

39. J. B. Andrews to J. P. Chamberlain, Oct. 6, 1916, AALL Papers.

40. "Industrial Health Insurance," *Boston Med. & Surg. J.,* 1916, *175:* 873.

41. "Medical Aspects of Social Insurance," ibid., p. 917. See also "Industrial Health Insurance," ibid., p. 541; and "The Doten Bill," ibid., 835.

42. Charles L. Upton, Letter to the Editor, ibid., 1917, *176:* 40. Upton was from Shelburne Falls. For other protests against compulsory health insurance, see Thomas F. Gunning, Letter to the Editor, ibid., 1916, *175:* 956-57; and "Abstract of Remarks of Dr. C. E. Mongan on Health Insurance before the Council of the Massachusetts Medical Society, Dec. 20, 1916," ibid, 1917, *176:* 35-39. Mongan, a Somerville practitioner, saw compulsory health insurance as "practically an [unfair] indictment of the medical profession" for not taking better care of the poor.

43. "Workmen's Sickness Insurance and the Doctor," ibid., 1916, *175:* 880-81.

44. Special Meeting of the Council, Dec. 20, 1916, ibid., 1917, *176:* 34.

45. John R. Commons, "Social Insurance and the Medical Profession," *Wisconsin Med. J.,* 1915, *13:* 301-6; W. F. Zierath, "The Socialization of Medicine," ibid., pp. 306-11.

46. T. J. Redelings, "Annual Address of the President," ibid., 1915, *14:* 186. See also the editorial "Health Insurance," ibid., 1916, *15:* 23-24.

47. Proc. House of Delegates, Oct. 3-6, 1916, ibid., p. 218.

48. Louis Jermain, "Annual Address of the President," ibid., pp. 140-41.

49. Report of the Health Insurance Committee, Oct. 4, 1916, ibid., pp. 226-28.

50. Proc. House of Delegates, Oct. 5, 1916, ibid., p. 283.

51. Ibid., p. 288.

52. Proc. Medical Society of the State of Pennsylvania, Sept. 18-21, 1916, *Penn. Med. J.,* 1916, *20:* 135, 143.

53. Francis D. Tyson, Discussion following papers on "Organization of Medical Service under Health Insurance," *ALLR,* 1917, *7:* 57.

54. On developments in California, see Arthur J. Viseltear, "Compulsory Health Insurance in California, 1915-18," *J. Hist. Med.,* 1969, *24:* 151-82.

55. "In Support of Health Insurance," *Calif. State J. Med.,* 1916, *14:* 346. See also "Industrial Sickness Insurance," ibid., 1915, *13:* 214; "Social Insurance," ibid., p. 456; "Take Warning! Health Insurance," ibid., 1916, *14:* 170. Bine is identified as the author of these editorials in Viseltear, "Compulsory Health Insurance in California," p. 159.

56. Ibid., 1916, *14:* 223.

57. "Social Insurance," ibid., pp. 302-3; "Health Insurance," ibid., p. 389.

58. Minutes of the Council on Health and Public Instruction, Oct. 28, 1916, AMA Archives.

59. René Bine, "Social Insurance," *Calif. State J. Med.,* 1916, *14:* 306-7. For a typical speech by I. M. Rubinow, see "Health Insurance: The Next Step in Social Progress," *Berkeley Civic Bull.,* 1916, *5:* 48-59.

60. James L. Whitney, "Cooperative Medicine in Relation to Social Insurance," *Calif. State J. Med.,* 1916, *14:* 432-39.

61. John H. Graves, "Should the Medical Profession Plead in Favor of the Proposed Health Insurance Bill?" ibid., pp. 439-46.

62. Ibid., p. 444.

63. Donald M. Gedge, "The Proposed Social Health Insurance Act," ibid., pp. 446-47.

64. R[ené] B[ine], "Health Insurance," ibid., 1917, *15:* 3-4.

65. Social Insurance Commission of the State of California, "Transcript of the Public Hearings Held in San Francisco, Nov. 20-22, 1916," pp. 267-68, 291-92. From a copy in the Labor Management Documentation Center, Cornell University.

66. "Social Insurance," *Illinois Med. J.,* 1916, *30:* 364; "Social Insurance Report," ibid., p. 417.

67. Meeting of the West Side Branch of the Chicago Medical Society, Dec. 21, 1916, *Chicago Medical Recorder,* 1917, *39:* 57-76; Edward H. Ochsner, "Further Objections to Compulsory Health Insurance," *Wisconsin Med. J.,* 1918, *17:* 224.

68. Ibid., p. 228; "Biography of Dr. Edward H. Ochsner," *Bull.,* Linn County Med. Soc., 1937, *6:* 5.

69. Eden V. Delphey, "Compulsory Health Insurance from the Point of View of the General Practitioner," *New York State J. Med.,* 1916, *16:* 602. Among the state societies with health insurance committees by the end of 1916 were New York, Massachusetts, California, Connecticut, and Rhode Island. Regarding the last two, see the Minutes of the House of Delegates, Nov. 17, 1916, *Rhode Island Med. J.,* 1917, *1:* 23; and "Report of the Committee on Public Policy and Legislation," *Proc.,* Conn. State Med. Soc., 1916, pp. 31-33. The Texas Medical Association was also studying health insurance in 1916; see Pat Ireland Nixon, *A History of the Texas Medical Association, 1853-1953* (Austin: University of Texas Press, 1953), p. 296.

70. Delphey, "Compulsory Health Insurance from the Point of View of the General Practitioner," p. 602. Questions and answers have been juxtaposed for clarity.

CHAPTER 5

1. "Industrial Insurance," *JAMA,* 1916, *66:* 433.

2. "Cooperation in Social Insurance Investigation," ibid., pp. 1469-70.

3. "Industrial Insurance," p. 433.

4. Rupert Blue, "Some of the Larger Problems of the Medical Profession," *JAMA,* 1916, *66:* 1901.

5. "Report of the Committee on Social Insurance," ibid., pp. 1951-85; "Report of Reference Committee on Legislation and Political Action," ibid., pp. 2080-81. For state reaction to this report, see, e.g., "Social Insurance," *J. Missouri State Med. Assn.,* 1916, *13:* 398.

6. I. M. Rubinow, "Medical Services under Health Insurance," *Proc. Conf. on Social Insurance,* Dec. 5-9, 1916, Bull. U.S. Bureau of Labor Statistics No. 212 (Washington: Government Printing Office, 1917), p. 692.

7. I. M. Rubinow, "20,000 Miles over the Land: A Survey of the Spreading Health Insurance Movement," *Survey,* 1917, *37:* 631. The pamphlets on social insurance, also published in the *AMA Bulletin,* were: (1) "Workmen's Compensation Laws," from the Report of the Judicial Council of the AMA for 1915, 1,000 copies; (2) "Social Insurance," the Report of the Special Committee of the AMA for 1916, 2,000 copies; (3) "Health Insurance in

Relation to the Public Dispensary," by Dr. I. M. Rubinow, 3,000 copies; (4) "Health Insurance in Relation to Public Health," by Dr. I. M. Rubinow, 2,000 copies; (5) "Social Insurance," by Dr. I. M. Rubinow, 1,000 copies; (6) "Medical Organization under Health Insurance," by Dr. Alexander Lambert, 1,000 copies; and (7) "Statistics Regarding the Medical Profession," compiled by the Committee on Social Insurance, 1,000 copies. Report of the Council on Health and Public Instruction, June 4-8, 1917, *JAMA*, 1917, *68:* 1719-20. The rising cost of paper and the need for financial retrenchment eventually curtailed the committee's publishing activities; see Frederick Green to the Members of the Council on Health and Public Instruction, Dec. 16, 1916, AMA Archives.

8. I. M. Rubinow, "Health Insurance: The Next Step in Social Progress," *Berkeley Civic Bull.,* 1916, *5:* 49-50.

9. J. B. Andrews to AALL Members, May 1, 1916, AALL Papers.

10. J. B. Andrews to Mrs. Elizabeth M. Fiedler, June 19, 1916, ibid.; J. B. Andrews to J. C. Skemp, June 19, 1916, ibid.; *Report of the Social Insurance Commission of the State of California* (Sacramento: California State Printing Office, 1917), pp. 271-72.

11. J. B. Andrews to the Social Insurance Committee, Aug. 22, 1916, AALL Papers; Lloyd F. Pierce, "The Activities of the American Association for Labor Legislation in Behalf of Social Security and Protective Labor Legislation" (Ph.D. diss., Univ. of Wisconsin, 1953), pp. 266-67.

12. Alexander Lambert, "Medical Organization under Health Insurance," *ALLR,* 1917, *7:* 40-41.

13. Ibid., pp. 36-50.

14. General discussion following papers on "Organization of Medical Service under Health Insurance," ibid., pp. 51-60. Rubinow, too, was inclined to attribute physician opposition to a "misunderstanding" of health insurance. "Abstract of Dr. Rubinow's Address," *Bull. Medical and Chirurgical Faculty of Maryland,* 1917, *9:* 140.

15. Alexander Lambert, "Health Insurance and the Medical Profession," *JAMA,* 1917, *68:* 257-62; "Compulsory Health Insurance," ibid., p. 292. The editorial erroneously stated that the AALL's model bill had "properly left blank the section providing for medical services, while asking the assistance of the medical profession to work out this phase of the problem." In a letter to the editor (ibid., p. 390) John Andrews pointed out that the third draft of the bill had already incorporated Lambert's principles for medical service under health insurance.

16. W. D. Chapman, Letter to the Editor, ibid., pp. 566-67. See also J. B. Andrews, Letter to the Editor, ibid., p. 729; and W. D. Chapman, Letter to the Editor, ibid., p. 797.

17. Albert Bowen, Letter to the Editor, ibid., p. 797.

18. George N. Jack, Letter to the Editor, ibid., p. 994.

19. A. B. Emmons, 2d, Letter to the Editor, ibid., pp. 651-52.

20. S. S. Goldwater, Letter to the Editor, ibid., p. 930.

21. John B. Andrews, Letter to the Editor, ibid., p. 994.

22. I. M. Rubinow, "Medical Services under Health Insurance," pp. 692-93.

23. "Statements of Prominent Persons in Favor of Health Insurance," *ALLR,* 1918, *8:* 324-27; B. S. Warren and Edgar Sydenstricker, *Health Insurance: Its Relation to the Public Health,* Public Health Bull. No. 76 (Washington: Government Printing Office, 1916); J. W. Schereschewsky, "Industrial Insurance," *JAMA,* 1914, *63:* 6. E. H. Lewinski-Corwin, executive secretary of the New York Academy of Medicine's Public Health Committee and a nonphysician, also strongly favored compulsory health insurance; see E. H. Lewinski-Corwin, "Health Insurance," *Medical Record,* 1916, *89:* 140, and "Notes and Suggestions concerning Health Insurance," MS dated Nov. 18, 1915, Records of the Public Health Committee, New York Academy of Medicine.

24. "Endorsement of Health Insurance by Health Authorities," *JAMA,* 1916, *67:* 832-33;

Alice Hamilton, "Health and Labor," *Survey,* 1916, *37:* 135-37. At a meeting in December, 1916, the Connecticut Public Health Association endorsed compulsory health insurance; "Jottings," ibid., p. 501.

25. "Health Insurance," *Am. J. Public Health,* 1916, *6:* 344-45.

26. See, e.g., John R. Commons and A. J. Altmeyer, "The Health Insurance Movement in the United States," *Report of the Health Insurance Commission of the State of Illinois* (Printed by the State, 1916), p. 643.

27. B. S. Warren, "Sickness Insurance: A Preventive of Charity Practice," *JAMA,* 1915, *65:* 2056-59; General discussion of papers on "Social Insurance," *ALLR,* 1916, *6:* 28-30; Alexander Lambert, "Organization of Medical Benefits and Services under the Proposed Sickness (Health) Insurance System," *Proc. Conf. on Social Insurance,* pp. 652-53, 702-06. See also B. S. Warren to J. B. Andrews, July 9, 1914, AALL Papers; B. S. Warren, "Health Insurance: Its Relation to the National Health," *JAMA,* 1916, *67:* 1015-19; and B. S. Warren, "Health Insurance: Its Relation to the Medical Profession," *Southern Med. J.,* 1917, *10:* 222-29.

28. Lambert, "Organization of Medical Benefits and Services," p. 653.

29. "Statements of Prominent Persons in Favor of Health Insurance," pp. 325-26.

30. Ibid.

31. Michael M. Davis, Jr., "The Dispensary's Place in Sickness Insurance," *Modern Hospital,* 1916, *6:* 134. Davis, a sociologist, was a member of the Committee on Social Insurance of the American Hospital Association. For this committee's activities, see ibid., 1917, *8:* 35; and 1917, *9:* 275, 438.

32. Minutes of the Ohio State Eclectic Medical Association, June 19-20, 1916, *Eclectic Med. J.,* 1916, *76:* 421; *Proc. Conf. on Social Insurance,* pp. 725-26.

33. Hills Cole to the California Social Insurance Commission, Oct. 17, 1916, *Report of the Social Insurance Commission of the State of California,* pp. 272-73.

34. See, e.g., the *Eclectic Med. J.,* 1915, *75:* 418; and 1916, *76:* 202, 244.

35. "Health Insurance," *Am. J. Nursing,* 1916, *17:* 188; Report of the Committee on Health Insurance, ibid., 1917, *17:* 864.

36. Martha M. Russell, "What Social Insurance Will Mean to Nurses," ibid., 1917, *17:* 391-92.

37. "Social Insurance," ibid., p. 385.

38. J. H. Beal, "Concerning Proposed Health Insurance Legislation," *Midland Druggist & Pharm. Rev.,* 1917, *51:* 306-16; J. H. Beal, "Some Objections to Compulsory Health Insurance," ibid., 1918, *52:* 107-16; Editorial introduction to Jesse S. Phillips, "The Menace of Compulsory Health Insurance in a Republic," ibid., 1917, *51:* 511; Harry B. Mason, "What Compulsory Health Insurance Would Mean to the Druggists," *J. Am. Pharm. Assn.,* 1917, *6:* 881-90. See also the Report of the Special Committee on Compulsory Health Insurance of the Chicago Branch of the American Pharmaceutical Association, ibid., pp. 314-17; and "Proceedings of the Local Branches: Detroit," ibid., p. 569.

39. I. M. Rubinow, "20,000 Miles over the Land," p. 632.

40. "Health Insurance Officially Endorsed," *ALLR,* 1917, *7:* 208-25.

41. "Federal Insurance Inquiry Proposed," *Survey,* 1916, *35:* 714; "Health Insurance before Congress," ibid., 1916, *36:* 115; *Commission to Study Social Insurance and Unemployment: Hearings before the Committee on Labor, House of Representatives, 64th Congress, First Session, on H.J. Res. 159, April 6 and 11, 1916* (Washington: Government Printing Office, 1918). For a summary of federal activities regarding health insurance, see Odin W. Anderson, "Health Insurance in the United States, 1910-1920," *J. Hist. Med.,* 1950, *5:* 373-74.

42. *Commission to Study Social Insurance and Unemployment,* p. 129. Gompers cited a recent statement by Surgeon General William C. Gorgas attributing his famous victory

over disease along the Panama Canal more to increased wages than to dead mosquitoes. "Add to the laboring man's wages from $1.25 to $2.50 a day," said Gorgas, "and you will lengthen the average American thread of life by 13 years at least."

43. Quoted in Bernard Mandel, *Samuel Gompers: A Biography* (Yellow Springs, Ohio: Antioch Press, 1963), p. 185.

44. Philip Taft, *The A. F. of L. in the Time of Gompers* (New York: Harper & Brothers, 1957), p. 365; Irwin Yellowitz, *Labor and the Progressive Movement in New York State, 1897-1916* (Ithaca, N.Y.: Cornell University Press, 1965), pp. 137-38. Among the New York labor leaders who favored compulsory health insurance were John Mitchell, John Lynch, and James Holland, president of the State Federation of Labor.

45. Ibid., pp. 19-21.

46. J. B. Andrews to J. C. Skemp, June 19, 1916, AALL Papers.

47. The statement of purpose appeared in many of the *Bulletins.*

48. Extracts from Frederick L. Hoffman's Talk at the National Civic Federation, Jan., 1917, recorded stenographically by Irene Sylvester, AALL Papers.

49. F. L. Hoffman to Irving Fisher, Dec. 11, 1916, ibid. See also F. L. Hoffman, "Some Fallacies of Compulsory Health Insurance," *Scientific Monthly*, 1917, pp. 306-16.

50. F. L. Hoffman to Irving Fisher, Feb. 5, 1917, AALL Papers.

51. Discussion, *Proc. Conf. on Social Insurance*, pp. 625-32, 695.

52. Olga S. Halsey to Irving Fisher, April 7, 1917, Fisher Collection, Yale University Library.

53. Irving Fisher to F. L. Hoffman, Dec. 19, 1916, and Feb. 9, 1917, AALL Papers.

54. Discussion at the annual meeting of the Wisconsin State Medical Society, Oct. 4, 1918, *Wisconsin Med. J.*, 1918, *17:* 232.

55. Minutes of the Social Insurance Dept., Dec. 20, 1916, quoted in Hace Sorel Tishler, *Self-Reliance and Social Security, 1870-1917* (Port Washington, N.Y.: Kennikat Press, 1971), p. 178.

56. F. L. Hoffman, *Facts and Fallacies of Compulsory Insurance* (Newark: Prudential Press, 1917), pp. 87-91.

57. "Compulsory Health Insurance: An American View," *Suppl. British Med. J.*, Aug. 25, 1917, pp. 51-52.

58. Hoffman, *Facts and Fallacies of Compulsory Insurance*, p. 86.

59. On the NCF and its activities, see Marguerite Green, *The National Civic Federation and the American Labor Movement, 1900-1925* (Washington: Catholic University Press, 1956); and James Weinstein, *The Corporate Ideal in the Liberal State, 1900-1918* (Boston: Beacon Press, 1968).

60. *New York Times*, March 13, 1916, p. 18; J. B. Andrews to J. P. Chamberlain, Oct. 6, 1916, AALL Papers.

61. J. W. Sullivan, Arthur Williams, and P. Tecumseh Sherman, *Report of the Committee on Preliminary Foreign Inquiry* (New York: National Civic Federation, 1914), pp. 33-34, 99.

62. I. M. Rubinow, "P's and Q's of Social Insurance," *Survey*, 1915, *34:* 183.

63. Olga S. Halsey, "An American Report on British Social Insurance: J. W. Sullivan, Arthur Williams and P. Tecumseh Sherman for the National Civic Federation," ibid., 1915, *33:* 695-96. See also J. W. Sullivan, Arthur Williams, and P. Tecumseh Sherman, Letter to the Editor, ibid., 1915, *34:* 177-78; and Olga S. Halsey, Letter to the Editor, ibid., pp. 178, 185.

64. Irving Fisher, "The Need for Health Insurance," *ALLR*, 1917, *7:* 19; "General Discussion," ibid., pp. 119, 128.

65. Hoffman, *Facts and Fallacies of Compulsory Insurance*, p. 47.

66. I. M. Rubinow, *Standards of Health Insurance* (New York: Henry Holt, 1916), p. 262.

CHAPTER 6

1. According to Odin W. Anderson, "Health Insurance in the United States, 1910-1920," *J. Hist. Med.*, 1950, *5:* 369, the following state legislatures considered the AALL's model bill or a similar proposal in 1917: California (a constitutional amendment), Colorado, Connecticut, Illinois, Maine, Massachusetts, Michigan, Minnesota, New Hampshire, New Jersey, New York, Ohio, Oregon, Pennsylvania, Washington, and Wisconsin.

2. "Doctors Discuss Forced Insurance," *New York Times*, Jan. 23, 1917, p. 3. Two of the papers read were William Gale Curtis, "The Economic Disadvantages of Compulsory Health Insurance," *New York State J. Med.*, 1917, *17:* 75-78; and Eden V. Delphey, "Compulsory Health Insurance," *Medical Record*, 1917, *91:* 357-61. For accounts of the meeting, see "Medical Society of the County of New York, Stated Meeting, Held Jan. 22, 1917," ibid., pp. 386-88; and "Symposium on Compulsory Health Insurance," *JAMA*, 1917, *68:* 801-4.

3. *Medical Record*, 1917, *91:* 388. In response to Curtis's charge that compulsory health insurance was "un-American," Samuel Kopetzky replied that if it were "un-American because it is compulsory, then compulsory education, compulsory vaccination, compulsory income tax are all, also un-American"; Kopetzky, "Comments on the Arguments of Mr. William Gale Curtis," *New York State J. Med.*, 1917, *17:* 80.

4. *Medical Record*, 1917, *91:* 386. Davin identifies himself as the author of this resolution in a Letter to the Editor, ibid., p. 468.

5. "Against Health Insurance," *New York Times*, Feb. 16, 1917, p. 20.

6. Ibid.

7. "Medical Society of the County of New York, Adjourned Meeting, Held Feb. 14, 1917," *Medical Record*, 1917, *91:* 388-92.

8. Ibid., p. 392.

9. Ibid., p. 391.

10. Medical Society of the County of Livingston, Regular Meeting, Mount Morris, Jan. 2, 1917, *New York State J. Med.*, 1917, *17:* 103.

11. Medical Society of the County of Washington, Special Meeting, Greenwich, Jan. 4, 1917, ibid., p. 155.

12. Medical Society of the County of Albany, Special Meeting, Albany, Jan. 10, 1917, ibid., p. 102.

13. Medical Society of the County of Schenectady, Regular Meeting, Schenectady, Jan. 16, 1917, ibid., pp. 155-56; "Medical Society of the County of Schenectady," *Albany Medical Annals*, 1917, *38:* 96-97.

14. Medical Society of the County of Monroe, Special Meeting, Rochester, Jan. 23, 1917, *New York State J. Med.*, 1917, *17:* 103. Two months later the society voted to oppose even the appointment of a state health insurance commission; Minutes of the Med. Soc. County of Monroe, March 20, 1917, Cornell University Archives.

15. Minutes of the Chautauqua County Med. Soc., Feb. 8, 1917, ibid.; Medical Society of the County of Cayuga, Regular Meeting, Auburn, Feb. 9, 1917, *New York State J. Med.*, 1917, *17:* 156; Dutchess-Putnam Medical Society, Special Meeting, Poughkeepsie, Feb. 12, 1917, ibid., p. 154; Medical Society of the County of St. Lawrence, Special Meeting, Ogdensburg, Feb. 13, 1917, ibid., p. 155; Richmond County Medical Society, Regular Meeting, St. George, Feb. 14, 1917, ibid., p. 154; Medical Society of the County of Erie, Regular Meeting, Buffalo, Feb. 19, 1917, ibid., p. 154; Minutes of the Council, Med. Soc. County of Kings, March 14, 1917, Archives of the Brooklyn Academy of Medicine. The Brooklyn physicians passed an anti-insurance resolution they had received from Floyd M. Crandall, secretary of the state medical society.

16. Minutes of the Chautauqua County Med. Soc., Feb. 8, 1917.

17. John V. Woodruff, Letter to the Editor, *JAMA*, 1917, *68:* 796. See also Joseph S.

Lewis, Letter to the Editor, ibid., pp. 797-98; and "Health Insurance Economics," *Buffalo Med. J.,* 1917, *72:* 517. Woodruff was chairman of the Committee on Economics of the Erie County Medical Society.

18. H. G. W[ebster], "Health Insurance: A Brief Review of the Proposed Act," *Long Island Med. J.,* 1917, *11:* 19.

19. Broome County Medical Society, Special Meeting, Binghamton, Jan. 9, 1917, *New York State J. Med.,* 1917, *17:* 156.

20. Minutes of the Council, Med. Soc. County of Kings, March 14, 1917.

21. Report of the Committee on Legislation, *New York State J. Med.,* 1917, *17:* 234.

22. "Urge More Study of Health Insurance," *New York Times,* March 8, 1917, p. 7. The *Times* reported the "widest possible divergence of opinions as to the merits and demerits of the Mills bill," with both labor and medicine hopelessly split.

23. John P. Davin, "Compulsory Health Insurance," *American Med.,* 1917, *23:* 188-92. The editors of *American Med.,* who generally supported compulsory health insurance, published Davin's address to air both sides of the issue; Editorial, "Compulsory Health Insurance Legislation," ibid., pp. 154-55. On Davin, see "The Death of Dr. John P. Davin," ibid., 1923, *29:* 620.

24. John D. Bonnar, "Compulsory Health Insurance Bill (Mills')," *Buffalo Med. J.,* 1917, *72:* 472-74.

25. "Health Insurance Plan," *New York Times,* March 13, 1917, p. 13; *New York Senate Journal,* 140th Session, 1917, *1:* 42-43. William S. Coffey introduced a similar bill in the Assembly but was equally unsuccessful; *New York Assembly Journal,* 140th Session, 1917, *1:* 336-37, 742.

26. Report of the Committee on Legislation, *Medical Record,* 1917, *91:* 742.

27. Report of the Committee on Medical Economics, *New York State J. Med.,* 1917, *17:* 237-38.

28. Ibid., p. 238.

29. Report of the Committee on Medical Economics, *Medical Record,* 1917, *91:* 743-44. This report lists fifteen "fundamentals" that would safeguard the profession; among them are adequate representation on administrative bodies, open panels, a limitation on the size of panels, free choice of physician, and fees based on the prevailing rates in any given community.

30. Minutes of the House of Delegates, *New York State J. Med.,* 1917, *17:* 256.

31. Ibid.

32. "Explanatory," ibid., pp. 159-60.

33. Report of the Committee on Public Health and Medical Education, *Medical Record,* 1917, *91:* 742.

34. For the provisions of the bill, see Commonwealth of Massachusetts, House No. 1074, bill accompanying the petition of Michael M. Davis, Jr., and others for the establishment of insurance against sickness, Social Welfare, Jan. 16, 1917, copy in the Davis Collection, New York Academy of Medicine.

35. "The Medical Provisions of the Young Bill," *Boston Med. & Surg. J.,* 1917, *176:* 174-75.

36. Frank E. Bateman, Letter to the Editor, ibid., p. 446.

37. Ibid.; "The Massachusetts Health Insurance Committee," ibid., p. 176; David L. Edsall to the President of the Massachusetts Medical Society, March 25, 1917, ibid., pp. 551-52. For Edsall's views on compulsory health insurance, see also his "Movements in Medicine," ibid., 1916, *174:* 893-94.

38. Bateman, Letter to the Editor, ibid., 1917, *176:* 446.

39. Stated Meeting of the Council, Massachusetts Medical Society, Feb. 7, 1917, ibid., pp. 285-89.

40. Annual Meeting of the Council, Massachusetts Medical Society, June 12, 1917, ibid., pp. 911, 917.

41. Edmund D. Chesebro, "Thirty Years Spent in the Study and Practice of Medicine," *Rhode Island Med. J.,* 1917, *1:* 152-53. On attitudes in Rhode Island, see also "Health Insurance," ibid., pp. 21-22; and "The Protest against Industrial Health Insurance," *Boston Med. & Surg. J.,* 1917, *176:* 280.

42. "Report of the Committee on Compulsory Health Insurance of the San Francisco County Medical Society," *Calif. State J. Med.,* 1917, *15:* 125.

43. Report of Committee on Compulsory Health Insurance, Medical Society of the State of California, April, 1917, ibid., pp. 197-98.

44. "Society Proceedings," *Wisconsin Med. J.,* 1917, *15:* 387. See also "Society Proceedings," ibid., p. 297; and "Society Proceedings," ibid., p. 341.

45. "Compulsory Health Insurance: The Sheep and the Goats," ibid., pp. 434-35.

46. A. W. Gray, "Compulsory Health Insurance," ibid., pp. 483-84.

47. "An Explanation," ibid., pp. 482-83.

48. Minutes of the House of Delegates, May 10, 1917, *Illinois Med. J.,* 1917, *32:* 58.

49. See, e.g., "Social Insurance: Its Bearing on the Profession and the Public as Observed in Great Britain and on the Continent," *JAMA.,* 1917, *68:* 396-98; and George Thomas Palmer, "Health Insurance from the Standpoint of the Physician," *Illinois Med. J.,* 1917, *31:* 5-9.

50. Edward H. Ochsner, "Some Objections to Health Insurance Legislation," ibid., pp. 77-81; E. H. Ochsner, "Further Objections to Compulsory Health Insurance," *Wisconsin Med. J.,* 1918, *17:* 224.

51. "Objections to Compulsory Health Insurance," *Illinois Med. J.,* 1917, *31:* 189. Many American physicians seem to have seen prohibition as the answer to compulsory health insurance. "When booze is stamped out in Pennsylvania," said the president of the state medical society, "there will be no occasion for health insurance, and medical and surgical services will be paid for per se." Walter F. Donaldson, "Health Insurance," *Penn. Med. J.,* 1918, *22:* 63. For similar statements, see "The Answer," ibid., 1919, *22:* 323; Eden V. Delphey, Letter to the Editor, *JAMA,* 1917, *68:* 1500; and "Discussion," *Wisconsin Med. J.,* 1918, *17:* 234.

52. Report of the Committee on Medical Legislation, *Illinois Med. J.,* 1917, *32:* 48.

53. Minutes of the House of Delegates, May 10, 1917, ibid., p. 59.

54. The medical societies of both North and South Carolina appointed committees on social insurance; but, though the president of the North Carolina society spoke favorably of health insurance, neither committee seems to have done much. Charles O'H. Laughinghouse, President's Address, Medical Society of the State of North Carolina, *Trans.,* 1917, pp. 19-20; Minutes of the House of Delegates, ibid., p. 378; C. B. Earle, President's Address, *J. South Carolina Med. Assn.,* 1917, *13:* 572; Minutes of the House of Delegates, ibid., 1918, *14:* 184. The president of the state medical society in Arizona, where a health insurance bill was killed in committee, expressed his opposition to insurance "because it is an undesirable form of practice which would bring us no respect and would lower our profession to that of a wage-earner." Robt. Ferguson, "Industrial Insurance," *Southwestern Med.,* 1917, *1:* 48-52.

CHAPTER 7

1. "The Springfield Meeting," *Illinois Med. J.,* 1918, *33:* 332. Over 600 of the 2,300 members of the Medical Society of the State of California joined the armed services during World War I; Report of the Secretary, April 16, 1918, *Calif. State J. Med.,* 1918, *16:* 345. About

3,700 of New York's 15,000 physicians entered military service; President's Report, Medical Society of the State of New York, *Medical Record*, 1919, *95:* 843. By 1917 some U.S. physicians were already serving in Europe.

2. I. M. Rubinow to George Derby, Jan. 18, 1926, Rubinow Papers. The committee office was closed in May, 1917.

3. Thomas Neville Bonner, *American Doctors and German Universities: A Chapter in International Intellectual Relations, 1870-1914* (Lincoln: University of Nebraska Press, 1963), p. 158.

4. Clara Eve Schieber, *The Transformation of American Sentiment toward Germany, 1870-1914* (Boston: Cornhill Pub. Co., 1923), p. xiii. See also Cushing Strout, *The American Image of the Old World* (New York: Harper & Row, 1963), p. 158.

5. On American prejudice during the war, see Harry N. Scheiber, *The Wilson Administration and Civil Liberties, 1917-1921* (Ithaca, N.Y.: Cornell University Press, 1960), pp. 51-59.

6. Arthur S. Link, *American Epoch: A History of the United States since the 1890's,* 2d ed. (New York: Alfred A. Knopf, 1963), p. 209; John C. Burnham, *Psychoanalysis and American Medicine, 1894-1918* (New York: International Universities Press, 1967), pp. 48-49.

7. See, e.g., Ernestine Black to J. B. Andrews, June 29, 1918, AALL Papers.

8. Arthur Dean Bevan, "The Organization of the Medical Profession for War," *JAMA,* 1918, *70:* 1809.

9. Minutes of the Medical Society of the County of Kings, April 16, May 15, May 21, June 27, Oct. 3, Oct. 15, 1918, Archives of the Brooklyn Academy of Medicine.

10. Frank E. Rowe, "Health Insurance," *J. Maine Med. Assn.,* 1918, *9:* 36, 47. The last comment was made by George H. Coombs.

11. Thomas W. Huntington, "Address of the President," American Surgical Assn., *Trans.,* 1918, *36:* 5-6. See also Ralph S. Cone, Letter to the Editor, *JAMA,* 1917, *68:* 2001-2.

12. Walter F. Donaldson, "Health Insurance," *Penn. Med. J.,* 1918, *22:* 62.

13. Discussion of Papers by Drs. McAllister, Donaldson, Van Sickle, and Others, ibid., p. 74.

14. Warren S. Stone, "Compulsory Health Insurance Legislation," *Medical Insurance and Health Conservation,* 1918-19, *28:* 219.

15. A. E. Forest, "Compulsory Health Insurance," *Wisconsin Med. J.,* 1918, *16:* 354.

16. Henry J. Harris to J. B. Andrews, March 12, 1918, AALL Papers.

17. William Green to J. B. Andrews, March 12, 1918, ibid.

18. Ibid.

19. J. R. Commons, "Health Insurance," *Wisconsin Med. J.,* 1918, *17:* 222.

20. Frederick L. Hoffman, *Failure of German Compulsory Health Insurance—A War Revelation* (Newark: Prudential Press, 1918). See also F. L. Hoffman, *Autocracy and Paternalism vs. Democracy and Liberty* (Newark: Prudential Press, 1918).

21. New Jersey Commission on Old Age, Insurance, and Pensions, *Report on Health Insurance* (1917), p. 1.

22. "The Soldiers' and Sailors' Insurance Law," *JAMA,* 1917, *69:* 1697; John B. Andrews, "Labor Laws in the Crucible: Measures Necessary for Effectiveness during and after the War," *Survey,* 1918, *39:* 544; Allen F. Davis, "Welfare, Reform and World War I," *American Quart.,* 1967, *19:* 523.

23. Ibid., pp. 524-25.

24. "Labor Getting Behind Health Insurance," *Survey,* 1918, *39:* 708-09; John B. Andrews, "Report of Work, 1918," *ALLR,* 1919, *9:* 162-63.

25. Elting E. Morrison (ed.), *The Letters of Theodore Roosevelt* (Cambridge: Harvard University Press, 1954), *8:* 1294.

26. "Hiram Johnson Urges Health Insurance Laws," *ALLR,* 1918, *8:* 320.

27. For an excellent account of the California debate, see Arthur J. Viseltear, "Compulsory Health Insurance in California, 1915-18," *J. Hist. Med.,* 1969, *24:* 151-82. The California vote was on a constitutional amendment to permit the establishment of a health insurance system.
28. J. B. Andrews to Barbara Nachtrieb, April 7, 1917, AALL Papers. See also "Objections to the California Plan Urged by Mr. Joseph P. Chamberlain in a Letter to Miss Nachtrieb, March 27, 1917," ibid.
29. "Problems and Methods of Legislative Investigating Commissions: Round Table Conference," *ALLR,* 1918, *8:* 100.
30. Committee of the Los Angeles Medical Society, "Tentative Report on Social Insurance," *Calif. State J. Med.,* 1918, *16:* 73.
31. Quoted in the Report of the Committee on Health Insurance, April 16, 1918, ibid., p. 348.
32. René Bine, "Present Status of Health Insurance in California," ibid., pp. 4-5.
33. Minutes of the House of Delegates, April 16, 1918, ibid., p. 344.
34. Report of the Committee on Health Insurance, April 16, 1918, ibid., p. 349.
35. Minutes of the House of Delegates, April 16, 1918, ibid., pp. 353-54.
36. On the League, see Wallace I. Terry, "California's League for the Conservation of Public Health," ibid., 1925, *23:* 1419-23; and "Proceedings of the Conference of Secretaries of Constituent State Medical Associations," *AMA Bull.,* 1922, *16:* 41-42.
37. "Social Health Insurance," *Calif. State J. Med.,* 1918, *16:* 510.
38. "Social Insurance," ibid., p. 474.
39. Report of the Committee on Health Insurance, April 16, 1918, p. 349; Notarized statement of Ernest Jerome Hopkins, San Francisco, Feb. 2, 1920, AALL Papers. According to Hopkins, Frederick Hoffman collaborated with the society but remained independent.
40. Ernestine W. Black to J. B. Andrews, Dec. 5, 1918, AALL Papers.
41. Ibid.
42. *Report of the Special Committee on Social Insurance,* Jan. 1, 1919 (Madison: Democrat Printing Co., 1919), pp. 33-34. Although this was a Wisconsin report, it accurately reflected the position of Christian Scientists in California and elsewhere in the United States.
43. Report of the Committee on Health Insurance, April 16, 1918, p. 349.
44. Black to Andrews, Dec. 5, 1918. Arthur J. Viseltear attributes the California defeat to "the fierce anti-intellectualism engendered in America as a result of the war" and to the belief that "compulsory" insurance was "un-American" because it deprived individuals of their personal freedom; Viseltear, "Compulsory Health Insurance in California," p. 181.
45. H. G. W[ebster], "Health Insurance Again," *Long Island Med. J.,* 1918, *12:* 188.
46. "Health Insurance Bill as Developed from 'Tentative Drafts,'" *ALLR,* 1919, *9:* 209; *New York Senate Journal,* 141st Session, 1918, *1:* 174, 264, 270, 332.
47. S. S. Goldwater to Henry Lyle Winter, March 23, 1918, AALL Papers; "The Growth of the Insurance Idea," *American Med.,* 1918, *24:* 196-97.
48. Goldwater to Winter, March 23, 1918.
49. "Legislative Notes," *New York State J. Med.,* 1918, *18:* 158. Henry Lyle Winter told the committee that he had corresponded with every medical society in the state and that they were unanimously opposed to the bill. For evidence of this opposition, see the Minutes of the Comitia Minora, Med. Soc. County of Monroe, March 5, 1918, Cornell University Archives; Minutes of the Tompkins County Med. Soc., March 19, 1918, ibid.; Minutes of the Dutchess County Medical Club, March 25, 1918, ibid.; Minutes of the Chautauqua County Med. Soc., May 26, 1918, ibid.
50. Report of the Committee on Legislation, *New York State J. Med.,* 1918, *18:* 231.
51. Report of the Committee on Medical Economics, ibid., pp. 231-36; Minutes of the

House of Delegates, May 21, 1918, ibid., p. 246. The delegates refused to endorse a substitute health insurance plan, offered by the Committee on Medical Economics, which would have given only cash benefits.

52. Report of the Committee on Health Insurance, *Boston Med. & Surg. J.,* 1918, *179:* 34.

53. "Ups and Downs of Health Insurance," *Survey,* 1918, *39:* 547.

54. "Notes Taken at a Hearing before the Special Commission on Social Insurance at the State House, Boston, Sept. 26, 1917," *Boston Med. & Surg. J.,* 1917, *177:* 603.

55. Ibid. For an exception, see John F. Martin, "The Social Insurance Cauldron," *American Med.,* 1917, *23:* 697-702. Martin was from Boston.

56. Report of the Committee on Social Insurance, *Wisconsin Med. J.,* 1918, *16:* 280-82. See also the address of the chairman of the committee, A. W. Gray, "Health Insurance," ibid., pp. 459-62.

57. Report of the Committee on Social Insurance, ibid., 1919, *17:* 306.

58. H. E. Dearholt, Discussion of papers by Commons and Ochsner, ibid., p. 232. Dearholt was executive secretary of the Wisconsin Anti-Tuberculosis Association. See also the comments by P. H. McGovern, ibid., p. 232.

59. Morris Fishbein, *A History of the American Medical Association, 1847 to 1947* (Philadelphia: W. B. Saunders, 1947), p. 297.

60. Minutes of the 68th Annual Session of the AMA, June 4-8, 1917, *JAMA,* 1917, *68:* 1755, 1832.

61. Charles H. Mayo, "War's Influence on Medicine," ibid., p. 1674.

62. "Compulsory Health Insurance," *New York Med. J.,* 1917, *106:* 33.

63. Frederick R. Green, Letter to the Editor, *Illinois Med. J.,* 1917, *32:* 32. Green was responding to Eugene T. Lies, Letter to the Editor, ibid., 1917, *31:* 420.

CHAPTER 8

1. J. B. Andrews to Republicans in the New York State Legislature, March 4, 1919, AALL Papers.

2. *New York Times,* Jan. 2, 1919, p. 4.

3. Irene Sylvester Chubb, "Memorandum on History of New York Health Insurance Campaign of 1919," AALL Papers; "Health Insurance Bills in New York State," *Medical Record,* 1919, *95:* 287.

4. Ibid.; *New York Times,* April 2, 1919, p. 1.

5. Minutes of the Med. Soc. County of Monroe, Feb. 26, 1919, Cornell Univ. Archives. See also "New York Doctors Oppose Health Insurance," *Medical Record,* 1919, *95:* 412; "Special Meeting, March 4, 1919," *Albany Medical Annals,* 1919, *40:* 158; and the resolutions appearing in the *New York State J. Med.,* 1919, *19:* 111-13.

6. Ibid., pp. 111, 113.

7. Minutes of the Tompkins County Med. Soc., March 25, 1919, Cornell Univ. Archives.

8. "Medical Society of the County of New York, Stated Meeting, Held Feb. 24, 1919," *Medical Record,* 1919, *95:* 506-8.

9. Minutes of the Med. Soc. County of Kings, Feb. 24, 1919, Archives of the Brooklyn Academy of Medicine.

10. H. G. W[ebster], "The Professional Guild," *Long Island Med. J.,* 1919, *13:* 193. The guild idea later spread to other New York counties and even to other states; H. G. W[ebster], "Medical Legislation," ibid., 1921, *15:* 65. See also "Professional Guild Organized against Health Insurance," *Medical Record,* 1919, *96:* 382; and Charles J. Whalen, "The Medical Profession Safeguarding Americanism," *J. Iowa State Med. Soc.,* 1921, *11:* 158-59.

11. Luther C. Payne to C. E. Scofield, Dec. 21, 1918, Records of the Med. Soc. County of Kings, Archives of the Brooklyn Academy of Medicine.

12. James J. Walsh, *History of Medicine in New York* (New York: National Americana Society, 1919), *5:* 366-67.

13. Quoted in a form letter to AALL members, *circa* Nov., 1918, AALL Papers. The "Russian disciple" was undoubtedly Rubinow.

14. Peter G. Filene, *Americans and the Soviet Experiment, 1917-1933* (Cambridge: Harvard University Press, 1967), p. 59 *et passim.*

15. Robert K. Murray, *Red Scare: A Study in National Hysteria, 1919-1920* (Minneapolis: University of Minnesota Press, 1955), p. 167.

16. William P. Cunningham, "A Bolshevik Bolus," *New York Med. J.,* 1918, *108:* 1061-65, 1113-16. The first part of this article was reprinted under the title "Socialistic Subjugation of the Medical Profession," in Chicago's *Medical Standard,* 1919, *42:* 21-25; Omaha's *Western Med. Rev.,* 1919, *24:* 121-32; and the *Delaware State Med. J.,* 1919, *10:* 8-18.

17. J. P. Warbasse, "Medical Reconstruction," *Long Island Med. J.,* 1919, *13:* 124-35. For Warbasse's views on compulsory health insurance, see "Additional Endorsements of Health Insurance," *ALLR,* 1919, *9:* 175.

18. H. G. W[ebster], "The Physician's Relation to the Social Problem," *Long Island Med. J.,* 1919, *13:* 313.

19. Harris A. Houghton, "'Medical Reconstruction': A Partial Answer," ibid., pp. 248-54. See also Robert E. Coughlin, "Health Insurance from the Physician's Standpoint," ibid., pp. 403-6; and "Minutes of the Twenty-Second Annual Meeting of the Associated Physicians of Long Island," ibid., 1920, *14:* 181-83.

20. "Medical Society of the State of New York, 113th Annual Meeting, Held in Syracuse, May 5-8, 1919," *Medical Record,* 1919, *95:* 846.

21. J. B. Andrews to J. P. Chamberlain, March 22, 1919, AALL Papers.

22. Chubb, "Memorandum"; *New York Times,* March 17, 1919, p. 20; ibid., March 20, 1919, p. 5.

23. George W. Kosmak to J. B. Andrews, March 12, 1919, AALL Papers.

24. Irene Sylvester Chubb to J. B. Andrews, March 12, 1919, ibid.

25. "One of Those Doubtful Signs," *Survey,* 1920, *43:* 369.

26. J. B. Andrews to New York Members of the AALL, Nov. 3, 1919, AALL Papers. Andrews' figures may have been low. A Long Island physician not at all sympathetic to compulsory health insurance estimated $1.00 for visits and 50 cents for office calls, adding up to $1,500 annually; John Joseph Kindred, "The Proposed Compulsory Health Insurance Law: Its Injustice to Physicians, Dentists, and Pharmacists," *Medical Record,* 1919, *96:* 1051.

27. "A Symposium on Compulsory Health Insurance," *Long Island Med. J.,* 1919, *13:* 434.

28. M. Schulman to J. B. Andrews, Feb. 22, 1919, AALL Papers.

29. "A Symposium on Compulsory Health Insurance," p. 434.

30. Grant C. Madill, "President's Address," *New York State J. Med.,* 1920, *20:* 97.

31. "Health Insurance Bill as Developed from 'Tentative Drafts,'" *ALLR,* 1919, *9:* 232-33; Thomas H. Halsted, "President's Annual Report," *New York State J. Med.,* 1919, *19:* 217.

32. E. MacD. Stanton, "Compulsory Health Insurance and Its Dangers," *Medical Record,* 1919, *96:* 751. One assemblyman received "stacks of letters" from doctors opposing the bill and only one letter from a physician supporting it; I. S. Chubb to J. B. Andrews, March 17, 1919, AALL Papers.

33. Halsted, "President's Annual Report," p. 217.

34. Chubb, "Memorandum"; John P. Davin, Letter to the Editor, *Medical Record,* 1919, *95:* 748.

35. Chubb, "Memorandum."

36. J. B. Andrews to J. P. Chamberlain, March 22, 1919, AALL Papers. The "Johnny-on-the-spot" reference comes from J. B. Andrews to Alexander Lambert, Feb. 19, 1919, ibid.

37. Andrews to Chamberlain, March 22, 1919; J. B. Andrews to John A. Lapp, March 21,

1919, ibid.; J. B. Andrews to Emma B. Beard, April 24, 1919, ibid.

38. James F. Rooney to H. L. Ames, April 12, 1919, ibid.

39. Chubb, "Memorandum,"; "Health Insurance as Developed from 'Tentative Drafts,'" pp. 236-37.

40. J. B. Andrews to AALL Members in New York, April 11, 1919, AALL Papers.

41. Chubb, "Memorandum"; *New York Times,* April 11, 1919, p. 4.

42. Chubb, "Memorandum"; "Health Insurance as Developed from 'Tentative Drafts,'" pp. 237-38. The other welfare bills provided for municipal ownership, hydro-electric power, a minimum wage, and an eight-hour day.

43. *New York Times,* April 18, 1919, p. 1.

44. J. B. Andrews to Frederick Almy, April 23, 1919, AALL Papers.

45. "Medical News," *Albany Medical Annals,* 1919, *40:* 393.

46. "Is Compulsory Health Insurance Inevitable?" *American Med.,* 1919, *25:* 674. This is a letter to the editor from the Committee on Public Information, Medical Society of the County of Schenectady.

47. Report of the Committee on Legislation, *New York State J. Med.,* 1919, *19:* 227.

48. Ibid.; Robert E. Coughlin, Letter to the Editor, *Long Island Med. J.,* 1919, *13:* 255.

49. John P. Davin, Letter to the Editor, *Medical Record,* 1919, *95:* 749.

50. Minutes of the House of Delegates, May 5, 1919, *New York State J. Med.,* 1919, *19:* 213.

51. Ibid., p. 208.

52. Medical Society of the County of Erie, Regular Meeting, Buffalo, April 21, 1919, ibid., p. 247.

53. Ibid., pp. 247-48.

54. Report of the Committee on Medical Economics, *Medical Record,* 1919, *95:* 845; Minutes of the Chautauqua County Med. Soc., April 18, 1919, Cornell Univ. Archives. On Sept. 30 the Chautauqua physicians rescinded their endorsement.

55. Medical Society of the County of Rensselaer, Special Meeting, Troy, April 29, 1919, *New York State J. Med.,* 1919, *19:* 198; Medical Society of the County of Washington, Semi-Annual Meeting, Comstock, May 13, 1919, ibid., p. 250.

56. H. P. Hourigan, Discussion, Symposium on Health Insurance, *Penn. Med. J.,* 1920, *23:* 205-6.

57. "Symposium on Compulsory Health Insurance," pp. 425-36.

58. Ibid., pp. 444-48; Minutes of the Med. Soc. County of Kings, Oct. 21, 1919, Archives of the Brooklyn Academy of Medicine; "Symposium on Compulsory Health Insurance and Allied Dangers," *Illinois Med. J.,* 1921, *39:* 309. The fifth speaker, a homeopathic physician named William L. Heeve, also denounced compulsory health insurance but without O'Reilly's eloquence.

59. F. M. Crandall, "The Special Meeting of the House of Delegates," *New York State J. Med.,* 1919, *19:* 201. The "ethical" problem of the 1880s concerned the proper relationship to assume with homeopathic doctors.

60. Columbia County Medical Society, Annual Meeting, Hudson, Oct. 7, 1919, ibid., p. 439; "Opposition to State Health Insurance," *Medical Record,* 1919, *96:* 732.

61. Medical Society of the County of Erie [sic], Oswego, Nov. 18, 1919, *New York State J. Med.,* 1919, *19:* 439.

62. Special Meeting of the House of Delegates, Medical Society of the State of New York, Nov. 22, 1919, ibid., pp. 401-7. The first part of the quotation is taken from an abridged version of the report appearing in *JAMA,* 1919, *73:* 1706.

63. Special Meeting of the House of Delegates, Nov. 22, 1919, p. 404; Alexander Lambert to J. B. Andrews, Dec. 12, 1919, AALL Papers.

64. Murray, *Red Scare,* pp. 191-244; Filene, *Americans and the Soviet Experiment,* pp. 61-62.

NOTES TO PAGES 95-98

65. J. B. Andrews to I. M. Rubinow, March 25, 1920, AALL Papers.
66. I. M. Rubinow to J. B. Andrews, Feb. 22, 1920, ibid.
67. H. G. W[ebster], "Senate Bill No. 1111," *Long Island Med. J.,* 1920, *14:* 187.
68. J. B. Andrews to Orlo J. Price, March 25, 1920, AALL Papers. See also *New York Times,* March 12, 1920, p. 12.
69. Ibid., April 8, 1920, p. 11.
70. Alexander Lambert to J. B. Andrews, Dec. 18, 1919, AALL Papers.
71. John B. Andrews, "Report of Work, 1919," *ALLR,* 1920, *10:* 73-74; Frederick MacKenzie, "The Legislative Campaign in New York for the 'Welfare Bills,'" ibid., pp. 139-40, 147-48; Olga S. Halsey to Marion Dickerman, Jan. 3, 1920, AALL Papers.
72. Alexander Lambert to Mrs. Gordon Norrie, April 2, 1920, ibid.
73. Albert T. Lytle to Alexander Lambert, March 30, 1920, ibid.
74. AALL correspondence, previously filled with talk of compulsory health insurance, rarely mentioned it after mid-1920.
75. Report of the Committee on Legislation, *New York State J. Med.,* 1921, *21:* 209; *New York Times,* Feb. 22, 1921, p. 2.
76. Henry Lyle Winter, "Social Insurance," *New York State J. Med.,* 1920, *20:* 20.

CHAPTER 9

1. Report of the Council on Health and Public Instruction, AMA, *JAMA,* 1920, *74:* 1242.
2. "Tocsin Calls Physicians in Five States to War against Health Insurance," *Illinois Med. J.,* 1920, *38:* 374. The Midwestern societies also kept in touch with the physicians of New York and New Jersey.
3. Editor's Report, ibid., 1922, *42:* 69-70. In 1922 the circulation of the journal was 7,600.
4. See, e.g., "By the New Editor," ibid., 1919, *36:* 87-90; "Deport Them Why Not?" ibid., pp. 200-203; and "Health Insurance Propaganda Not Dead," ibid., 1920, *38:* 36-37.
5. "State Medicine Destroys Individual Initiative and Will Nullify Medical Progress the Same as Compulsory Health Insurance Has Done in Germany," ibid., 1921, *39:* 68.
6. Report of the Committee on Health Insurance, ibid., 1920, *38:* 151-53; "Health Insurance a National Fraud," ibid., 1919, *35:* 92-94.
7. "Get Together Meeting of Doctors, Dentists and Druggists," ibid., 1921, *39:* 149; "Symposium on Compulsory Health Insurance and Allied Dangers," ibid., pp. 293-309. In 1922 Ochsner, nominated by Whalen, was elected president of the Illinois State Medical Society, ibid., 1922, *42:* 72.
8. Report of Committee on Industrial and Civic Relations, *J. Indiana State Med. Assn.,* 1920, *13:* 323; "Compulsory Health Insurance," ibid., pp. 90-91; Editorial, ibid., 1922, *15:* 174.
9. Edward H. Ochsner, "Compulsory Health Insurance: A Modern Fallacy," *J. Michigan State Med. Soc.,* 1920, *19:* 283-88; "Illinois Loans Michigan Battery of Speakers," *Illinois Med. J.,* 1920, *37:* 274-75; Minutes of the House of Delegates, AMA, April 26-30, 1920, *JAMA,* 1920, *74:* 1256. The Michigan journal also reprinted O'Reilly's Chicago address; "Symposium on Compulsory Health Insurance and Allied Dangers," *J. Michigan State Med. Soc.,* 1921, *20:* 173-88.
10. George Frothingham, "Compulsory Health Insurance," *Detroit Med. J.,* 1920, *21:* 179; "Illinois Loans Michigan Battery of Speakers," p. 274.
11. Edward H. Ochsner, "Further Objections to Compulsory Health Insurance," *Wisconsin Med. J.,* 1918, *17:* 224-30; Report of the Committee on Social Insurance, ibid., 1920, *18:* 283.

The Minnesota State Medical Association apparently never took a stand on compulsory health insurance, although it did invite Hoffman to address its annual meeting in 1920 and its Committee on Social Insurance clearly regarded health insurance as a "menace." See Frederick L. Hoffman, "Compulsory Health Insurance and the Medical Profession," *Minnesota Medicine,* 1921, *4:* 63-68; and the Reports of the Committee on Social Insurance, ibid., 1920, *3:* vi-vii; 1921, *4:* viii; 1922, *5:* vii-viii.

Thomas Neville Bonner notes that Kansas physicians had also grown hostile to health insurance by 1920: "From tentativeness, even mild approval of some system of health insurance before the War, medical groups became increasingly sharp in their criticisms and reservations after the war." Bonner, *The Kansas Doctor: A Century of Pioneering* (Lawrence: University of Kansas Press, 1959), pp. 224-25.

12. Minutes of the House of Delegates, Medical Society of the State of Pennsylvania, Oct. 4-7, 1920, *Penn. Med. J.,* 1921, *24:* 109.

13. Report of the Committee on Health Insurance, *Proc.,* Conn. State Med. Soc., 1920, pp. 52-53.

14. John R. Commons and A. J. Altmeyer, "The Health Insurance Movement in the United States," *Report of the Health Insurance Commission of the State of Illinois* (1919), p. 642; Minutes of the House of Delegates, AMA, June 6-10, 1921, *JAMA,* 1921, *76:* 1756; S. Rubinow to J. B. Andrews, Jan. 9, 1920, AALL Papers; John P. Davin, "The Legislative History of Compulsory Health Insurance in the State of New York," *Medical Record,* 1920, *97:* 107. It is not clear from Rubinow and Davin whether the New Jersey State Medical Society actually passed a resolution against health insurance or merely expressed its virtually unanimous hostility.

15. W. S. Rankin, "State Medicine," *Trans.,* Med. Soc. State of N. Carolina, 1920, pp. 282-83. Rankin himself was not opposed to health insurance.

16. John A. Lapp, "The Findings of Official Health Insurance Commissions," *ALLR,* 1920, *10:* 27-40; Odin W. Anderson, "Health Insurance in the United States, 1910-1920," *J. Hist. Med.,* 1950, *5:* 372. In 1917 the New Hampshire legislature voted to create a commission, but the project was apparently never funded; see Harry Alvin Millis, *Sickness and Insurance* (Chicago: University of Chicago Press, 1937), p. 119.

17. Olga S. Halsey, "The British National Insurance Act and the New York Health Insurance Bill Compared," March, 1920, AALL Papers.

18. See, e.g., Lapp, "The Findings of Official Health Insurance Commissions," p. 33; Ohio Health and Old Age Insurance Commission, *Health, Health Insurance, Old Age Pensions* (Columbus: F. J. Heer Printing Co., 1919), pp. 194-95; *Report of the Health Insurance Commission of the State of Illinois,* pp. 164, 172; *Report of the Special Committee on Social Insurance* (Madison: Democrat Printing Co., 1919), pp. 41-42.

19. Frederick L. Hoffman, *National Health Insurance and the Medical Profession* (Newark, N.J.: Prudential Press, 1920), pp. iii-xv. Among Hoffman's other pamphlets, all published by the Prudential Press, are: *Failure of German Compulsory Health Insurance—A War Revelation* (1918), *Facts and Fallacies of Compulsory Health Insurance* (1919), *Health Insurance and the Public* (1919), *National Health Insurance and the Friendly Societies* (1920), *Poor Law Aspects of National Health Insurance* (1920), and *Address on the Methods and Results of National Health Insurance in Great Britain* (n.d.).

After the war Hoffman joined the Committee on Foreign Inquiry of the National Civic Federation's Social Insurance Department, which was continuing its prewar efforts to discredit compulsory health insurance. See the following publications by the National Civic Federation: J. W. Sullivan and Others, *Second Report of the Committee on Foreign Inquiry* (1920), *A Refutation of False Statements in Propaganda for Compulsory Health Insurance* (1919), and *Compulsory Sickness Insurance* (1920).

20. "The Failure of German Compulsory Health Insurance," *JAMA,* 1919, *72:* 348.

21. Comments on the activities of Mr. Frederick Hoffman, taken from interviews by Alzada Comstock, Dec., 1919, AALL Papers. See also Alfred Cox to J. B. Andrews, July 30, 1920, ibid.

22. "An American View of the National Insurance Scheme," *British Med. J.,* Sept. 18, 1920, pp. 444-45.

23. Discussion, Symposium on Health Insurance, March 14, 1919, *Penn. Med. J.,* 1919, *22:* 676-77.

24. These letters, all written between Nov. 3, 1919, and Feb. 18, 1920, were solicited by the Public Health Committee of the New York Academy of Medicine and are preserved among its records. On Oct. 2 Sir Arthur Newsholme had told the Academy that the Health Insurance Act was "generally condemned" in England; "The Increasing Socialization of Medicine," *Survey,* 1920, *43:* 360.

25. John B. Andrews, "Representative Opinion of Health Insurance in Great Britain," *ALLR,* 1921, *11:* 105; J. B. Andrews to James M. Lynch, July 19, 1919, AALL Papers.

26. W. A. Appleton to J. B. Andrews, Aug. 22, 1919, ibid.; Arthur Henderson to J. B. Andrews, Aug. 25, 1919, ibid.; Michael Heseltine to J. B. Andrews, Aug. 25, 1919, ibid.; W. S. Turner [?] to J. B. Andrews, Aug. 27, 1919, ibid.

27. Alfred Cox to J. B. Andrews, Aug. 20, 1919, ibid.

28. Joseph P. Chamberlain, "A Personal View of Health Insurance in England," *ALLR,* 1921, *11:* 94.

29. William T. Ramsey and Ordway Tead, "Report of Investigation into the Operation of the British Health Insurance Act," ibid., p. 258. See also Ordway Tead, "Fact and Opinion as to the British National Health Insurance Act," ibid., pp. 87-93; and Alfred Cox's comments on Tead's article in a letter to J. B. Andrews, April 8, 1921, AALL Papers.

30. Alfred Cox, "Seven Years of National Health Insurance in England: A Retrospect," *JAMA,* 1921, *76:* 1308-12, 1350-53, 1397-1403; "National Health Insurance in England," ibid., pp. 1313-14; Alexander Lambert to J. B. Andrews, Nov. 4, 1920, AALL Papers.

31. "National Health Insurance in England Still an Experiment," *JAMA,* 1921, *77:* 1656-57. See, e.g., London Correspondent, "A Crisis in Panel Practice," ibid., p. 1349.

32. Hoffman, *Failure of German Compulsory Health Insurance,* p. 6.

33. "Health Insurance," *New York State J. Med.,* 1920, *20:* 398.

34. Alfred Cox assured J. B. Andrews that the information given him was "very similar" to what he had provided Hoffman; Cox to Andrews, April 9, 1920, AALL Papers.

35. Tead, "Fact and Opinion," p. 88.

36. Report of the Council on Health and Public Instruction, *JAMA,* 1919, *72:* 1750. This report also lists S. S. Goldwater as a member of the committee, but the records of the Council do not substantiate this; Minutes of the Council on Health and Public Instruction, Oct. 4, 1919, AMA Archives. On the views of M. L. Harris, see "National Health Insurance," *Illinois Med. J.,* 1919, *35:* 10-12.

37. I. M. Rubinow to J. B. Andrews, May 6, 1919, AALL Papers; I. M. Rubinow to J. B. Andrews, Feb. 22, 1920, ibid.

38. Report of the Council on Health and Public Instruction, p. 1750.

39. Minutes of the Board of Trustees, AMA, Feb. 7, 1919, AMA Archives.

40. Eden V. Delphey to H. E. Lomax, April 27, 1918, *Albany Medical Annals,* 1919, *39:* 235.

41. Minutes of the House of Delegates, *Illinois Med. J.,* 1919, *36:* 46, 50.

42. Minutes of the House of Delegates, *JAMA,* 1919, *72:* 1832.

43. Alexander Lambert, "Medicine: A Determining Factor in War," ibid., pp. 1713-21. Lambert used this occasion to call for the establishment of a National Department of Health, a measure considerably less controversial than health insurance.

44. Alexander Lambert to J. B. Andrews, Jan. 28, 1920, AALL Papers.

45. Minutes of the Executive Committee, Board of Trustees, AMA, Jan. 2, 1920, AMA Archives. Perhaps the most active letter writer was E. MacD. Stanton of Schenectady, New York, described by Andrews as "one of the most active opponents" of health insurance in the state; J. B. Andrews to Henry J. Harris, March 24, 1920, AALL Papers.

46. M. L. Harris, "Compulsory Health Insurance," *JAMA*, 1920, *74:* 907-8; M. L. Harris, "Effects of Compulsory Health Insurance on the Practice of Medicine," ibid., pp. 1041-42.

47. Eden V. Delphey to the County Medical Society Delegates attending the Annual Meeting of the Medical Society of the State of New York, March 18, 1920, Library of the New York Academy of Medicine; Eden V. Delphey to State Medical Society Delegates attending the New Orleans Session of the AMA, April 16, 1920, ibid.; Eden V. Delphey, "Report of the Committee on Compulsory Health and Workmen's Compensation Insurance of the Medical Society of the County of New York," *New York State J. Med.,* 1920, *20:* 394.

48. Delphey to State Medical Society Delegates, April 16, 1920; Minutes of the House of Delegates, Medical Society of the State of New York, March 23, 1920, *New York State J. Med.,* 1920, *20:* 136.

49. Quoted in "Tolerance," *Penn. Med. J.,* 1920, *23:* 475. The Pennsylvania journal deplored the intemperate language coming from Michigan and suggested that "Probably it was written after a strenuous day's work."

50. Report of the Council on Health and Public Instruction, 1920, *JAMA*, 1920, *74:* 1241-42.

51. Frederick R. Green, "The Social Responsibilities of Modern Medicine," *Trans.,* Med. Soc. State N. Carolina, 1921, pp. 401-03. This address was reprinted in *JAMA*, 1921, *76:* 1477-83. See also F. R. Green to George E. Frothingham, Nov. 17, 1919, *Illinois Med. J.,* 1920, *37:* 212; F. R. Green to the Editor, *J. Indiana State Med. Assn.,* 1920, *13:* 91; and F. R. Green, "Health Insurance—A Challenge to Physicians," *Penn. Med. J.,* 1921, *24:* 224-29. In May 1920, Edward H. Ochsner praised Green for delivering "a brilliant address" against compulsory health insurance; Discussion on Health Insurance, *Illinois Med. J.,* 1920, *38:* 93.

52. Minutes of the House of Delegates, *JAMA*, 1920, *74:* 1256.

53. "American Medical Association by Unanimous Resolution Condemns Health Insurance," *Illinois Med. J.,* 1920, *37:* 418-19.

54. Minutes of the House of Delegates, *JAMA*, 1920, *74:* 1319.

55. "American Medical Association by Unanimous Resolution Condemns Health Insurance," p. 419. Although he was the outgoing president of the AMA, Lambert was apparently not a delegate and thus technically not eligible to vote or to participate in floor discussions.

56. Alexander Lambert to J. B. Andrews, May 3, 1920, AALL Papers.

57. "It Is Strange, Dr. Lambert," *Illinois Med. J.,* 1920, *37:* 418.

58. Ibid.; "The History of the Towns' Lambert Drug and Booze Cure," ibid., 1920, *38:* 167-71; Minutes of the House of Delegates, ibid., p. 165. Two years later the Illinois delegation to the AMA secured the defeat of a candidate for Speaker of the House of Delegates on the basis of his friendship with Lambert; "Illinois' Part in the A.M.A. St. Louis Meeting," ibid., 1922, *42:* 61.

59. "The American Medical Association and Health Insurance," *Modern Medicine,* 1920, *2:* 406.

60. Edward T. Devine, "Doctors and Health Insurance," *Survey,* 1920, *44:* 526.

61. "Presidential Candidates and the Medical Profession," *Illinois Med. J.,* 1920, *38:* 449-50.

62. J. B. Andrews to AALL Members, Nov. 23, 1920, AALL Papers.

63. Alexander Lambert to J. B. Andrews, Nov. 27, 1920, ibid.

64. Report of the Committee on Health Insurance, Illinois State Medical Society, *Illinois Med. J.,* 1922, *42:* 76-77. See also E. V. D[elphey], Letter to the Editor, ibid., 1921, *39:* 280.

65. J. Stanley Lemons, "The Sheppard-Towner Act: Progressivism in the 1920s," *J. American Hist.,* 1969, *55:* 776-86.

66. John B. Andrews, "Report of Work," *ALLR*, 1922, *12:* 78.

67. "Doctor Write Your Senators and Congressmen at Once Opposing the Sheppard-Towner Maternity Bill Now in Congress," *Illinois Med. J.,* 1921, *39:* 143.

68. John H. Graves, "Some Accomplishments and Problems of the Medical Society of the State of California," *Calif. State J. Med.,* 1922, *20:* 180.

69. "Exposing the 'Con' in Social Economics, and Putting the A.M.A. on Record," *Illinois Med. J.,* 1921, *39:* 555.

70. Minutes of the 72nd Annual Session of the AMA, June 6-10, 1921, *JAMA,* 1921, *76:* 1682, 1756-57, 1763; F. H. McMechan to the Secretaries of the County Medical Societies, Ohio State Medical Association, *J. Indiana State Med. Assn.,* 1922, *15:* 25-26. According to John J. A. O'Reilly, the Massachusetts delegation also endorsed the condemnation of state medicine; Letter to the Editor, *Medical Record,* 1922, *101:* 550.

71. Minutes of the 72nd Annual Session of the AMA, pp. 1757-58. For Billings' changing views on compulsory health insurance, see "Statements of Prominent Persons in Favor of Health Insurance," *ALLR,* 1918, *8:* 324; Frank Billings, "The Future of Private Medical Practice," *JAMA,* 1921, *76:* 352; Frank Billings, "The Past, Present and Future Policies of the American Medical Association," *AMA Bulletin,* 1921, *15:* 412; "Socializing Medicine," *J. Indiana State Med. Assn.,* 1921, *14:* 428-29.

72. Editorial, ibid., p. 236.

73. John J. A. O'Reilly, Letter to the Editor, *Medical Record,* 1922, *101:* 550-51; Minutes of the Med. Soc. County of Kings, Feb. 21, 1922, Archives of the Brooklyn Academy of Medicine. These goals seem to have been shared by the "Medical Advisory Committee"; see "Resolutions Adopted by County Societies," *AMA Bulletin,* Jan. 15, 1922, *16:* 13-15.

74. Minutes of the 73rd Annual Session of the AMA, May 22-26, 1922, *JAMA,* 1922, *78:* 1715. Resolutions condemning state medicine were also introduced by the delegates from Illinois, Ohio, Maryland, and the District of Columbia.

75. John B. Andrews, "Report of Work," *ALLR,* 1923, *13:* 90.

76. Report of the Committee on Medical Economics, *New York State J. Med.,* 1925, *25:* 789. See, however, "Oregon Defeats Health Insurance," *Calif. & Western Med.,* 1925, *23:* 86.

77. On this second American debate over compulsory health insurance, see Daniel S. Hirshfield, *The Lost Reform: The Campaign for Compulsory Health Insurance in the United States from 1932-1943* (Cambridge: Harvard University Press, 1970).

EPILOGUE

1. John Gordon Freymann, "Leadership in American Medicine: A Matter of Personal Responsibility," *New England J. Med.,* 1964, *270:* 710-15. Freymann also acknowledges the role of external factors, like the disillusionment that followed World War I.

2. The data for 1916 are incomplete, but apparently fewer than one-fourth of the delegates in 1917 returned to the House of Delegates in 1920. *JAMA,* 1916, *66:* 1499-1500; 1917, *68:* 1354; 1920, *74:* 839-40. Academics are identified in the AMA's *American Medical Directory* for 1918 and 1921.

3. Ray Lyman Wilbur, "Human Welfare and Modern Medicine," *JAMA,* 1923, *80:* 1890-91.

4. Elton Rayack, *Professional Power and American Medicine: The Economics of the American Medical Association* (Cleveland: World Pub., 1967), pp. 143-146.

5. Carleton B. Chapman and John M. Talmadge, "The Evolution of the Right to Health Concept in the United States," *Pharos,* 1971, *34:* 39. A shortened version of this paper appeared under the title "Historical and Political Background of Federal Health Care

Legislation," *Law and Contemporary Problems,* 1970, *35:* 334-47. Michael M. Davis offers a similar explanation in *Medical Care for Tomorrow* (New York: Harper & Brothers, 1955), pp. 275-76.

6. On Harris, see Thomas Neville Bonner, *Medicine in Chicago, 1850-1950: A Chapter in the Social and Scientific Development of a City* (Madison, Wis.: American History Research Center, 1957), pp. 219-20.

7. On Webster's reasons for changing, see H. G. W., "Health Insurance and the National Civic Federation," *Long Island Med. J.,* 1920, *15:* 45.

8. For Van Sickle's later position, see "Special Session of the Homeopathic Medical Society of Pennsylvania for the Consideration of Compulsory Health Insurance," *Hahnemannian Monthly,* 1920, *55:* 747-53.

9. Charles H. Lemon, e.g., was a member of the society's pro-insurance Health Insurance Committee; yet in 1920 he applauded the AMA's resolution against compulsory health insurance. Report of Delegates to A.M.A., *Wisconsin Med. J.,* 1921, *19:* 391.

10. "Special Session of the Homeopathic Medical Society of Pennsylvania," pp. 737, 765. See also Charles E. Sawyer, "What Is the Doctor's Present Position?" *Eclectic Med. J.,* 1920, *80:* 182-85.

11. On the impact of the war on the Progressive movement, see Charles Hirschfield, "Nationalist Progressivism and World War I," *Mid-America,* 1963, *45:* 139-56; Herbert F. Margulies, "Recent Opinion on the Decline of the Progressive Movement," ibid., pp. 250-68; and Allen F. Davis, "Welfare, Reform and World War I," *American Quart.,* 1967, *19:* 516-33.

12. I. M. Rubinow, *The Quest for Security* (New York: Henry Holt, 1934), p. 214.

13. *Eighth Biennial Report of the Wisconsin Tax Commission* (Madison, Wis., 1916), p. 62; *Tenth Biennial Report of the Wisconsin Tax Commission* (Madison, Wis., 1920), p. 34. A survey of 2,316 Illinois physicians in 1918 or 1919 indicated that the average gross income was $4,617 for Chicago physicians, $5,490 for those practicing in Peoria, Springfield, and other cities with populations above 10,000, and $3,665 for those in smaller towns and rural areas. Only 6.4 percent of the state's physicians earned under $1,200, while 6.3 percent made $10,000 or more. *Report of the Health Insurance Commission of the State of Illinois* (Springfield: Illinois State Journal, 1919), pp. 78-79.

14. *Historical Statistics of the United States, 1789-1945* (Washington: Government Printing Office, 1949), pp. 50, 236.

15. During this same period many American physicians were also discovering what it was like to work for the government—in the U.S. Army.

16. On the early history of workmen's compensation in America, see Harry Weiss, "The Development of Workmen's Compensation Legislation in the United States," Ph.D. diss., Univ. of Wisconsin, 1933; and Roy Lubove, *The Struggle for Social Security, 1900-1935* (Cambridge: Harvard University Press, 1968), pp. 45-65.

17. *Workmen's Compensation Laws,* Social Insurance Series Pamphlet No. 1 (Chicago: AMA [1915]), p. 60. See also Ohio Health and Old Age Insurance Commission, *Health, Health Insurance, Old Age Pensions: Report, Recommendations, Dissenting Opinions* (1919), p. 424; and Proc. 10th Annual Conf. on Medical Legislation, *AMA Bulletin,* 1914, *9:* 151.

18. "The Side Door to Socialism," *JAMA,* 1952, *149:* 574.

19. Minutes of the Eighty-Fifth Annual Session, June 11-15, 1934, ibid., 1934, *102:* 2200. See also the address of President-Elect Dean Lewis, ibid., 1933, *100:* 2021.

20. Davis, *Medical Care for Tomorrow,* p. 276.

SOURCES FOR THE EPIGRAPHS

Chapter 1: Ohio Health and Old Age Insurance Commission, *Health, Health Insurance, Old Age Pensions: Report, Recommendations, Dissenting Opinions* (Columbus, 1919), pp. 131-32.

Chapter 2: Irving Fisher, "The Need for Health Insurance," *New York State J. Med.,* 1917, *17:* 84.

Chapter 3: F. R. Green to J. B. Andrews, Nov. 11, 1915, AALL Papers.

Chapter 4: "Opposition to the Health Insurance Bill," *Medical Record,* 1916, *89:* 424.

Chapter 5: (1) Rupert Blue, "Some of the Larger Problems of the Medical Profession," *JAMA,* 1916, *66:* 1901.

(2) "Cooperation in Social Insurance Investigation," *JAMA,* 1916, *66:* 1469-70.

Chapter 6: Eden V. Delphey, "Compulsory Health Insurance: A Criticism of the Tentative Draft and Its Promulgation," *Medical Record,* 1917, *91:* 357.

Chapter 7: (1) Quoted in "Social Insurance," *Calif. State J. Med.,* 1918, *16:* 474.

(2) George H. Coombs, Comments on Frank E. Rowe, "Health Insurance," *J. Maine Med. Assn.,* 1918, *9:* 47.

Chapter 8: (1) "A Symposium on Compulsory Health Insurance Presented before the Medical Society of the County of Kings, Oct. 21, 1919," *Long Island Med. J.,* 1919, *13:* 445.

(2) Ibid., pp. 431, 434.

Chapter 9: (1) Alexander Lambert to John B. Andrews, Jan. 28, 1920, AALL Papers.

(2) Report of the Committee on Medical Economics, *New York State J. Med.,* 1925, *25:* 789.

INDEX

INDEX

Agricultural states, 99
Albany, N.Y., 40, 66, 82, 90, 91
Albany County Medical Society (N.Y.), 66
Albany Medical Annals, 38
Alcoholics, 7, 106
Almshouses, 7
American Association for Labor Legislation: founding of, 15; membership of, 16; and phossy jaw, 16; and model bill, 20-21, 22, 25-26; investigates European plans, 21-22; 1916 campaign of, 37-51; opens legislative campaign, 37; meets physicians' demands, 42, 89; wartime criticism of, 77-78; 1918 campaign of 81; 1919 campaign of, 85; discouraged, 96; abandons campaign, 108-109
— Committee on Social Insurance: creation of, 16; work of, 18-21; mentioned, 35, 36
American Economic Association, 59
American Federation of Labor, 60
American Hospital Association, 24, 58
American Institute of Homeopathy, 58
American Journal of Nursing, 59
American Journal of Public Health, 57
American Medical Association: and Flexner report, 4; Judicial Council, 9, 23, 28, 33, 35, 102; Council on Health and Public Instruction. 26, 28, 33, 35, 36, 83, 103, 104; history of, 27-28; reorganization of, 28-29; House of Delegates, 28, 103, 104, 105, 107, 108, 110-11; Trustees, 28, 36, 103, 104, 108; Council on Medical Education, 28; Council on Pharmacy and Chemistry, 28; progressive outlook of, 29; attitude toward European insurance, 29; low membership of, 32; positive attitude toward insurance, 33, 52, 83; Committee on Social Insurance, 36, 52, 102, 104; Illinois resolution re, 73-74; anti-German feeling of, 76; ambivalence of, 83-84, 95; its four principles, 83, 103; votes against insurance, 105; and state medicine, 107-108; leaders of, 110, 112; mentioned, 18, 30, 31, 47, 50, 52, 75, 94, 114
— *Journal* of: 29-35 passim, 52, 56, 83, 100, 102, 106, 124 n.16, 126 n.40
American Medicine, 39, 134 n.23
American Nurses Association, 58
American Pharmaceutical Association, 59
American Public Health Association, 57
American Red Cross, 75
American Statistical Association, 17, 18

American Surgical Association, 77
Anderson, John F., 57
Andrews, John B.: photograph of, 15; becomes secretary of AALL, 15; and Committee on Social Insurance, 17; on physician attitudes toward insurance, 22-23, plans for 1916 campaign, 26; and F. R. Green, 33, 34; attends N.Y. hearings, 40; on Massachusetts doctors, 45; activities of, 54; quoted, 57, 79, 90, 91, 95, 106; testifies, 60; in England, 101, 102; mentioned, 21, 35, 61, 89, 92, 101, 104, 105, 114
Anti-Semitism, 88
Arizona State Medical Society, 135 n.54
Associated Manufacturers and Merchants of N.Y. State, 85
Associated Physicians of Long Island, 88
Association of Edison Illuminating Companies, 62
Atlantic City, N.J., 103
Austria, 10, 29
Automobile, 4

Babcock, C. D., 61, 81, 96
Bankers, 9
Barbat, J. Henry, 80
Beard, Mary, 44, 58, 71
Bellevue Hospital, 23
Berg, Henry W., 66, 68
Berlin correspondent, 29, 124 n.13
Bevan, Arthur Dean, 76
Billings, Frank, 30, 108, 112
Bine, René, 47, 80
Binghamton, N.Y., 67
Bismarck, Otto von, 10
Blue, Rupert, 52, 57
Bolshevism, 87, 88, 97, 98, 110
Bonnar, John D., 68
Boston, 44, 71, 72, 107, 108
Boston Dispensary, 44
Boston Medical and Surgical Journal, 45, 70
Braisted, William C., 110
Bremner, Robert, 19
Bristow, Algernon T., 31
British Medical Association: demands of, 11, 30-31; activity of, 32; position of, 101
British Medical Journal, 62, 100
Brook, J. D., 107
Brooklyn, N.Y., 77, 86, 88, 92, 93, 94, 108

151

Library of Congress Cataloging in Publication Data

Numbers, Ronald L
  Almost persuaded.

  (The Henry E. Sigerist supplements to the Bulletin of
the history of medicine; no. 1)
  Includes bibliographical references and index.
  1. Medicine, State—United States—History.
2. Insurance, Health—United States—History.
3. Physicians—United States—Attitudes. I. Title.
II. Series.
RA412.5.U6N86   368.4'2'0973   77-17254
ISBN 0-8018-2052-9